Longman Keys to Language Teaching

Teaching English to Children

Longman Keys to Language Teaching

Series Editor: Neville Grant

Teaching English to Children

Wendy A. Scott and Lisbeth H. Ytreberg

Longman

London New York

Longman Group UK Limited,
Longman House, Burnt Mill, Harlow,
Essex CM20 2JE, England
and Associated Companies throughout the world.

Published in the United States of America
by Longman Inc., New York

© Longman Group UK Limited 1990

First published 1990
Second impression 1991
British Library Cataloguing in Publication Data

Teaching English to children (Longman keys to language learning)
　1. Education. Curriculum subjects: English language.
Teaching 420.7

Library of Congress Cataloging in Publication Data

Scott, Wendy A.
　Teaching English to children/Wendy A. Scott, Lisbeth
　H. Ytreberg.
　　　p.　　　cm. – (Longman keys to language teaching)
　　　ISBN 0-582-74606-X
　　　1. English language – Study and teaching (Elemen-
tary) – Foreign speakers.　　2. Language arts
(Elementary) I. Ytreberg, Lisbeth H.
　　II. Title.　　III. Series.
　　　PE1128.A2S325　1990　372.65'21044 –– dc20

ISBN 0582 74606 X

Set in 10/12pt 'Monophoto' Century Schoolbook 227
Produced by Longman Singapore Publishers Pte Ltd
Printed in Singapore

We are grateful to the following for permission to
reproduce copyright material:

NKS-Forlaget for page 24 (bottom). Mary Glasgow
Publications Ltd for pages 92 and 94. Concari,
Rodriguez and Urrestarazu, Snap Pupils Book 1,
Heinemann Publishers (Oxford) Ltd for page 58.
Concari, Rodriguez, Urrestarazu and Barbisan, Snap
Activity Book 2, Heinemann Publishers (Oxford) Ltd
for pages 71 and 91 (top). © UP TO YOU 1 PLUS, Liber
AB, Sweden/Illustration by Ilon Wikland for page 62
(right). Oxford University Press for pages 25, 26, 27,
37 (bottom), 44 (bottom left) and 90 (bottom). From
THE NOSE BOOK by Al Perkins, illustrated by Roy
McKie. Copyright © 1970 by Random House, Inc.
Reprinted by permission of Random House, Inc for page 65
Material on pages 18, 21, 35 (bottom), 36 (top), 45
(bottom), 52, 53, 62 (left), 64 and 111 all taken from
books published by Longman Group UK Ltd.

Contents

Authors' note

We would like to thank Neville Grant for his perceptive and useful comments as this book was being written, as well as colleagues, pupils, family and friends who helped us by supplying material and making encouraging noises throughout the writing process. We would especially like to thank Jørgen Ytreberg for all his help with the art work.

Preface

THE TEACHING OF English to young children has become especially important in recent years. One reason for this has been the introduction of primary EFL teaching in a number of European countries – but it is also a world-wide phenomenon. There is a lot of very good teaching in primary EFL classrooms. However, it is a fact that many teachers now find themselves teaching in primary school even though they have not been trained for this level. And even for teachers who have been trained, there is a lack of good books concerning this important area of teaching.

This book is a resource book of ideas and approaches for use with young children. Wendy Scott and Lisbeth Ytreberg have wide experience in teacher training, mainly in Norway. Throughout the book, the writers remind us of what it is to be a child – and help us to adapt our styles of teaching to accommodate the needs and motivations of young learners.

Like the other books in the *Longman Keys to Language Teaching* series, *Teaching English to Children* offers sound, practical, down-to-earth advice on useful techniques and approaches in the classroom. This book contains lots of practical ideas for developing the four language skill areas, and illustrates how this work can be organised, and integrated, particularly by means of topic work. All the activities suggested here can be adapted and used with children anywhere, by any teacher.

Neville Grant

1 The young language learner

The British philosopher John Stuart Mill started to learn Greek at the age of three. Clearly, John Stuart Mill was not an average child. What we are talking about in this chapter is the average child. This book assumes that your pupils are between five and ten or eleven years old. This means that the book covers some of the most vital years in a child's development. All education, including learning a foreign language, should contribute positively to that development.

There is a big difference between what children of five can do and what children of ten can do. Some children develop early, some later. Some children develop gradually, others in leaps and bounds. It is not possible to say that at the age of five all children can do x, at the age of seven they can all do y, or that at the age of ten they can all do z. But it is possible to point out certain characteristics of young children which you should be aware of and take into account in your teaching. You, as the teacher, are the only one who can see how far up the ladder your individual pupils are. We can only draw your attention to the characteristics of the average child which are relevant for language teaching.

We have divided the children into two main groups throughout the book – the five to seven year olds and the eight to ten year olds. We are assuming that the five to seven year olds are all at level one, the beginner stage. The eight to ten year olds may also be beginners, or they may have been learning the foreign language for some time, so there are both level one and level two pupils in the eight to ten age group.

Five to seven year olds

What five to seven year olds can do at their own level

- They can talk about what they are doing.
- They can tell you about what they have done or heard.

- They can plan activities.
- They can argue for something and tell you why they think what they think.
- They can use logical reasoning.
- They can use their vivid imaginations.
- They can use a wide range of intonation patterns in their mother tongue.
- They can understand direct human interaction.

Other characteristics of the young language learner

- They know that the world is governed by rules. They may not always understand the rules, but they know that they are there to be obeyed, and the rules help to nurture a feeling of security.
- They understand situations more quickly than they understand the language used.
- They use language skills long before they are aware of them.
- Their own understanding comes through hands and eyes and ears. The physical world is dominant at all times.
- They are very logical – what you say first happens first. 'Before you turn off the light, put your book away' can mean 1 Turn off the light and then 2 put your book away.
- They have a very short attention and concentration span.
- Young children sometimes have difficulty in knowing what is fact and what is fiction. The dividing line between the real world and the imaginary world is not clear. When reading a story in a foreign language class of five year olds about a mouse that got lost, the teacher ended the story by saying, 'But, what's this in my pocket? I feel something warm and furry and it squeaks.' She then took a toy mouse out of her pocket accompanied by gasps from her pupils. They had no problem in believing that the mouse had found its way out of the book and into their teacher's pocket. They simply thought the teacher was wonderful because she had found the lost mouse!

- Young children are often happy playing and working alone but in the company of others. They can be very reluctant to share. It is often said that children are very self-centred up to the age of six or seven and they cannot see things from someone else's point of view. This may well be true, but do remember that sometimes pupils don't want to work together because they don't see the point. They don't always understand what we want them to do.

- The adult world and the child's world are not the same. Children do not always understand what adults are talking about. Adults do not always understand what children are talking about. The difference is that adults usually find out by asking questions, but children don't always ask. They either pretend to understand, or they understand in their own .terms and do what they think you want them to do.
- They will seldom admit that they don't know something either. A visiting friend took a confident five year old to school one day after the child had been going to school for three weeks. It was only when they arrived at a senior boys' school after forty-five minutes that the visitor realised that the child had no idea where she was. Her mother had asked her several times before she left home if she knew the way, the visitor had asked the same question several times in the forty-five minutes. The child had answered cheerfully and confidently that she knew the way to her school very well!
- Young children cannot decide for themselves what to learn.
- Young children love to play, and learn best when they are enjoying themselves. But they also take themselves seriously and like to think that what they are doing is 'real' work.
- Young children are enthusiastic and positive about learning. We all thrive on doing well and being praised for what we do, and this is especially true for young children. It is important to praise them if they are to keep their enthusiasm and feel successful from the beginning. If we label children failures, then they believe us.

Eight to ten year olds
General characteristics

Children of five are little children. Children of ten are relatively mature children with an adult side and a childish side. Many of the characteristics listed above will be things of the past.

- Their basic concepts are formed. They have very decided views of the world.
- They can tell the difference between fact and fiction.

- They ask questions all the time.
- They rely on the spoken word as well as the physical world to convey and understand meaning.
- They are able to make some decisions about their own learning.
- They have definite views about what they like and don't like doing.
- They have a developed sense of fairness about what happens in the classroom and begin to question the teacher's decisions.
- They are able to work with others and learn from others.

Language development

Eight to ten year olds have a language with all the basic elements in place. They are competent users of their mother tongue and in this connection they are aware of the main rules of syntax in their own language. By the age of ten children can:

- understand abstracts
- understand symbols (beginning with words)
- generalise and systematise.

This refers to children's general language development. When it comes to learning a foreign language, there is still a lot we do not know. There are many similarities between learning one's mother tongue and learning a foreign language in spite of the differences in age and the time available. So far nobody has found a universal pattern of language learning which everyone agrees with. Much seems to depend on which mother tongue the pupils speak and on social and emotional factors in the child's background. What is clear here is that most eight to ten year olds will have some sort of language awareness and readiness which they bring with them into the foreign language classroom.

The period from five to ten sees dramatic changes in children, but we cannot say exactly when this happens because it is different for all individuals. The magic age seems to be around seven or eight. At around seven or eight, things seem to fall into place for most children and they begin to make sense of the adult world as we see it.

DAD: Did you get a good place in the exams, Julie?
JULIE: Yes, Dad, next to the radiator.

Think about young children telling jokes. Five year olds laugh because everybody else does, but they don't always understand the joke. If they are asked to re-tell the joke it will be nonsense. Seven year olds think jokes are funny and they learn them off by heart. This means that they often get the punch line wrong or have to be prompted. Ten and eleven year olds remember jokes and can work out the punch line from the situation. The system of language and the understanding of it seems to fall into place for many children in the same way.

What this means for our teaching

Words are not enough

Don't rely on the spoken word only. Most activities for the younger learners should include movement and involve the senses. You will need to have plenty of objects and pictures to work with, and to make full use of the school and your surroundings. Demonstrate what you want them to do. The balance will change as the children get older, but appealing to the senses will always help the pupils to learn.

Play with the language

Let the pupils talk to themselves. Make up rhymes, sing songs, tell stories. Play with the language – let them talk nonsense, experiment with words and sounds: 'Let's go – pets go.' 'Blue eyes – blue pies.' Playing with the language in this way is very common in first language development and is a very natural stage in the first stages of foreign language learning too.

Language as language

Becoming aware of language as something separate from the events taking place takes time. Most eight to ten year olds already have this awareness in their own language. The spoken word is often accompanied by other clues to meaning – facial expression, movement, etc. We should make full use of these clues. When pupils start to read, the language becomes something permanent and there are fewer other clues to meaning. Pupils can take a book home, they can read it again and again, they can stop, think about the language and work it out. The same is true of writing. So reading and writing are extremely important for the child's growing awareness of language and for their own growth in the language, although both are very demanding and take time and patience to learn.

Variety in the classroom

Since concentration and attention spans are short, variety is a must – variety of activity, variety of pace, variety of organisation, variety of voice. We go into this in more depth in Chapter 8. Older pupils can concentrate for longer periods and you should allow them to do so, but you still need lots of variety.

Routines

Children benefit from knowing the rules and being familiar with the situation. Have systems, have routines, organise and plan your lessons. Use familiar situations, familiar activities. Repeat stories, rhymes, etc. Again we look more closely at these points in another chapter, this time Chapter 2 – Class management and atmosphere.

Cooperation not competition

Avoid rewards and prizes. Other forms of encouragement are much more effective – see also the comments on this subject on page 11. Make room for shared experiences – they are an invaluable source of language work and create an atmosphere of involvement and togetherness. Most of us enjoy the feeling of belonging and this is particularly true of young children.

Group the children together whenever possible. This does not mean that they have to work in groups all the time, but most children like to have other children around them, and sitting with others encourages cooperation. Genuine cooperative pairwork and groupwork is usually the result of a long process – see pages 15 to 17. Some pupils work best alone.

Grammar

Children have an amazing ability to absorb language through play and other activities which they find enjoyable. How good they are in a foreign language is not dependent on whether they have learnt the grammar rules or not. Very few of your pupils will be able to cope with grammar as such, even at the age of ten or eleven. They may be very aware and clear about the foreign language, but they are not usually mature enough to talk about it.

As a teacher, you should note the structures, functions and grammar items which you want your pupils to learn as well as those they already know, but your actual teaching should only include the barest minimum of grammar taught as grammar, and then for the older children only. This does not mean teaching grammar rules to the whole class. The best time to introduce some sort of simple grammar is either when a pupil asks for an explanation, or when you think a pupil will benefit from learning some grammar. This may be when you are correcting written work, or it may be in connection with an oral exercise which practises, for example, 'Did she . . .?' and 'Does she . . .?' Older pupils, especially those at level two, may ask exactly what the difference is between 'did' and 'does', since both are used for questions, and you can then use the opportunity to explain the difference in simple terms. You might want to use the terms 'a yesterday question' and 'a today question'. It might or might not be appropriate to compare what happens in the mother tongue in the same situation. What is important is that the explanations should be given on an individual/group basis when the pupils themselves are asking the questions, that the explanations are kept as simple as possible, and that the pupils are able to grasp the point and so benefit from the explanation.

Assessment

Even though formal assessment may not be a compulsory part of your work, it is always useful for the teacher to make regular notes about each child's progress. You may want to tell parents how their children are doing, and you should be talking to the children regularly about their work and encouraging self-assessment. From the beginning this can be done in very simple terms, stressing the positive side of things and playing down what the pupil has not been able to master. Nothing succeeds like success.

Questions and activities

1 Think back to when you went to school. What do you remember about your first years? Do you remember the teachers, the teaching, smells, sounds, your physical surroundings, other pupils, feelings? How do your memories fit in with what has been said in this chapter about learning in general?
2 Go back to your own learning days again, this time when you started learning a foreign language. Was it a good or a bad experience? Why? Can you draw any conclusions from it about what you should/should not do in your language classroom?

2 Class management and atmosphere

What is an ideal teacher?

These ten year olds have very definite ideas about what they like in a teacher.
Susan says,

My ideal school Teacher is mrJolly because I like his music

Darren says,

My ldeal teacher is funny and makes you work hard. and lets me draw things from my Innagination.

Terry would like

A patient teacher, and who doesn't mind children getting things wrong, sometimes. A teacher who enjoys fun and games.

And Anette says,

Is a strict teacher who is strict to the naughty children and nice to the good ones. And has always got chalk. handy.

Teachers come in all shapes and sizes.

We come to the job with our personalities already formed, but there are abilities and attitudes which can be learnt and worked on. As a teacher of young children it helps a lot if you have a sense of humour, you're open-minded, adaptable, patient, etc., but even if you're the silent, reserved type, you can work on your attitudes and abilities.

Abilities

We may not all be brilliant music teachers like Susan's Mr Jolly, but most of us can learn to sing or even play a musical instrument. All music teachers would agree in any case that everyone can sing, although perhaps not always in tune!

If you think you can't draw, have a look at Andrew Wright's book *1000 Pictures for Teachers to Copy* (Collins 1984)

We can all learn to mime, to act and to draw very simple drawings. We can all learn to organise our worksheets so that they are planned and pleasing to look at. And we can certainly all learn to have our chalk handy!

Attitudes

Respect your pupils and be realistic about what they can manage at an individual level, then your expectations will be realistic too.

As a teacher you have to appear to like all your pupils equally. Although at times this will certainly include the ability to act, the children should not be aware of it. Children learning a foreign language or any other subject need to know that the teacher likes them. Young children have a very keen sense of fairness.

It will make all the difference in the world if you yourself feel secure in what you are doing. Knowing where you are going and what you are doing is essential. You can build up your own security by planning, reading, assessing and talking to others. Hopefully this book will help you to know what you are doing.

Helping the children to feel secure

Once children feel secure and content in the classroom, they can be encouraged to become independent and adventurous in the learning of the language. Security is not an attitude or an ability, but it is essential if we want our pupils to get the maximum out of the language lessons.

Here are some of the things which will help to create a secure class atmosphere:

- As we said above, know what you're doing. Pupils need to know what is happening, and they need to feel that you are in charge (see Chapter 8 for a detailed discussion of how to plan).
- Respect your pupils. In the school twelve-year-old Gerd would like,

Peoples and teatchers whould be frends and they could speak to eats ather like frends.

- Whenever a pupil is trying to tell you something, accept whatever he or she says – mistakes as well. Constant, direct correction is not effective and it does not help to create a good class atmosphere. Correction has its place when you are working on guided language exercises, but not when you are using the language for communication. We talk about this again in the chapter on oral work.
- Just as Terry's ideal teacher is one 'who doesn't mind children getting things wrong, sometimes', ideal pupils shouldn't laugh at others' mistakes, and this has to be one of the rules of the class. Children of all ages are sometimes unkind to each other without meaning to be and are sometimes unkind to each other deliberately. Pupils have to

be told that everyone makes mistakes when they are learning a new language, and that it is all right.

- Establish routines: 'Good morning. It's Wednesday today, so let's hear your news.' Friday is the day you read the book of the month. Have a birthday calendar, so that you know when everybody's birthday is, and have a routine for what to do on that day. Have a weather chart so that the weather can be written up every day. Have a calendar with day, date and month. Routines of this type build up familiarity and security for both age groups.

- Give the children the responsibility for doing practical jobs in the classroom – making sure the calendar is right, sharpening the pencils, giving out the library books, watering the plants. These activities are genuine language activities and involve both taking responsibility for learning and helping others to learn.

- As we said in Chapter 1, avoid organised competition. Although it can be great fun and usually leads to a great deal of involvement, there is almost always a winner and a loser, or a winning team and a losing team. Language learning is a situation where everyone can win. Children compete naturally with each other – to see who's finished first etc., but this is something different.

- Avoid giving physical rewards or prizes. It tells others that they have not 'won' and it does not help learning to take place. It is far better to tell the pupil that you like his or her work, or put it up on the display board, or read the story aloud for the others or do whatever seems appropriate. This gives the pupil a sense of achievement which doesn't exclude the other pupils. Include, don't exclude.

- Don't give children English names. Language is a personal thing, and you are the same person no matter what language you are using.

Margaret Donaldson's book, *Children's Minds* (Collins 1978) has a lot of interesting things to say about the disadvantages of rewards.

The physical surroundings

Young children respond well to surroundings which are pleasant and familiar. If at all possible, put as much on the walls as you can – calendars, posters, postcards, pupils' drawings, writing etc. Have plants, animals, any kind of interesting object, anything which adds character to the room, but still leaves you space to work.

Encourage the children to bring in objects or pictures or postcards and tell the rest of the class a little bit about them in English. It doesn't have to be more than, 'This postcard is from Portugal. My aunt is in Portugal.' Physical objects are very important to young children, even children of ten.

Your classroom is probably used for other subjects or other classes as well, but try to have an English corner – you need shelves, a notice board, and either a pile of cushions or a couple of comfortable chairs (preferably not traditional school chairs). If you really can't manage even a corner of the classroom, a section of wall that you can pin things on is better than nothing.

Make sure you mark all your files and boxes so that you and your pupils know where to find what. Mark the boxes with colours and/or pictures as well as words. Pupils will respond to the organisation – it shows you care.

Arranging the desks

Sometimes you may not be able to change how the desks are
arranged in your classroom, and sometimes you may have to
make one arrangement which you can't change. You may want
to arrange the desks in different ways for different lessons, but
it is much simpler if you decide on the most suitable
arrangement for a lesson and stick to it. Moving desks during a
lesson is a very noisy and time-consuming business.

Let's look at three ways of arranging the desks in an ordinary
classroom.

Arrangement A

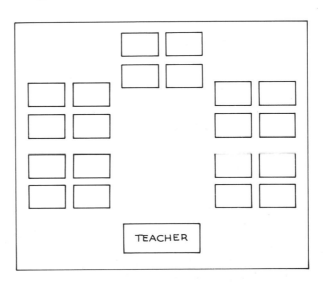

With Arrangement A, you can teach the whole class easily, and
you can have group work for some of the time, with the class
working in groups of four. It is good for pupils to sit in groups,
even if they are doing individual or class work, since it is then
much more natural for them to talk to each other.

Arrangement A also lets you do pairwork easily and leaves you
a space in the middle of the classroom for more general
activities. It gives you room to play games, tell stories, act out
dialogues, etc. The front of the classroom is not always the best
place for these activities if you want to create a feeling of
involvement rather than performance.

Arrangement B

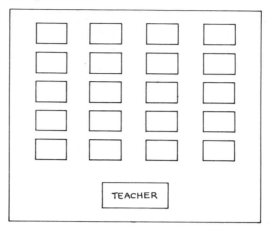

Arrangement B works for individual and whole class work, and you can easily do pairwork if half the class turn their backs to the teacher, or if half the pupils move their chairs over to their neighbour's desk. Arrangement B does not encourage natural communication since pupils can only see the back of the heads of the pupils in front of them, so it is not as suitable as Arrangement A for language work.

Arrangement C

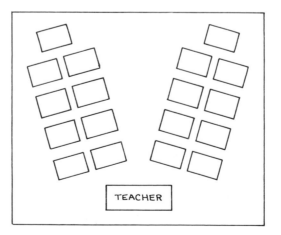

For more suggestions about classroom arrangements, see Mary Underwood's book *Effective Class Management* in the same series as this book – *Longman Keys to Language Teaching* (Longman 1987)

Arrangement C works in the same way as Arrangement B, But is more flexible and leaves you with space in the middle of the classroom.

Grouping the children

As we said in Chapter 1, it is important to keep in mind that not all children will take to pair and groupwork at once. Particularly five and six year olds are often happiest working alone, and are not yet willing to cooperate and share. They will want to keep all the cards, read the book alone, play with all the toys in the English corner, etc. Cooperation is something which has to be nurtured and learnt, so if your pupils have been to kindergarten or play school, or if they are already part of a class, then this may not be a problem at all.

If your pupils are sitting in groups of four most of the time, as in Arrangement A on page 13, you will find that although they are working as four individuals, they often develop a group identity. This type of arrangement makes it easier to see when pupils are ready to cooperate with other pupils, and we would recommend some sort of regular grouping, especially for the five to seven age range.

Pairwork

Pairwork is a very useful and efficient way of working in language teaching. It is simple to organise and easy to explain, and groupwork should not be attempted before the children are used to working in twos first.

- Let pupils who are sitting near each other work together. Don't move desks – and chairs should only be moved if absolutely necessary.
- Establish a routine for pairwork, so that when you say, 'Now work in your pairs', pupils know what is expected of them. The routine depends on how your classroom is arranged. If the pupils are sitting in rows as in Arrangement B, then it might be that all pupils sitting in rows 1 and 3 turn round to face rows 2 and 4, while those working in row 5 work with the person next to them.

- Pairwork means that everyone in the class is occupied, but even if everyone in the class is working on the same thing, not all pairs will finish at the same time. Do not be tempted to let the pairwork continue until everyone has finished. As soon as you see that several of the pairs have finished, ask the others to finish off and move back to their own seats.
- If you do not have an even number of pupils in the class, then let one group work as a three. If you always partner the odd pupil then you will not be able to help the others.
- Be on the lookout for pupils who simply do not like each other – it is unlikely that they will work well together. This is more of a problem with eight to ten year olds than it is with five to seven year olds.
- Go through what you want pupils to do before you put them into their pairs.

Groupwork

Everything which has been said about pairwork applies to groupwork. We cannot put children into groups, give them an exercise and assume that it will work.

Introducing groupwork

If your pupils are not used to working in groups in other classes or if they do not naturally develop a group identity, as they may do if they are sitting permanently in a group (Arrangement A), then you can introduce them gradually to groupwork.

1 Start by having teaching groups – groups which you teach separately from the rest of the class. This allows you to give some pupils more individual attention.
2 Then you can go on to introducing self-reliant groups – groups which are given something to do on their own, with the teacher only giving help when needed.
3 Start with just one group. Tell them clearly what the purpose is – 'I want you to make me a poster', and why they are working together – 'If there are four of you, you can help each other and share the work.'
4 Go through this process with all the groups before you let the whole class work in groups at the same time.

Numbers

Limit numbers in the group to between three and five.

Who works with whom?

Children should not be allowed to choose their groups, partly because this takes a lot of time, but mainly because it usually means that someone is left out. If your pupils sit in groups all the time, then it is natural for them to work most of the time in those groups. There is no reason why pupils should not be moved about from time to time.

Particularly with the eight to ten year olds, you might want to put them in mixed ability groups some of the time, but sometimes group them according to ability. Clever pupils can and do help the not so clever ones if the groups are mixed, but sometimes you want to give extra help to either the clever or the not so clever on their own.

Classroom Language

PUPIL 1: Can I borrow your pencil, please?
PUPIL 2: Yes.
PUPIL 1: Thanks.

TEACHER: What's this called in English? Anyone know? Guess! Juan, do you know?
JUAN: Sorry, I don't know.
TEACHER: Okay. Well, it's called jam.

PUPIL: Can I have a pair of scissors, please?
TEACHER: Of course. You know where they are – in the cupboard.
PUPIL: Thank you.

PUPIL 1: Whose turn is it to get the books?
PUPIL 2: Elvira's.
PUPIL 1: Your turn, Elvira.
ELVIRA: Okay.

If cooperation and communication are to be part of the process of learning a language as well as part of the process of growing up, then the sooner the pupils learn simple, meaningful expressions in English, the easier it will be. A very important way of helping pupils progress from dependence on the book and on the teacher to independence is to give them the necessary tools. One of the tools is classroom language.

For example, few children of five will admit that they don't know the answer to a question. Nor will they ask for more information if they don't understand what they have to do. Very often they will just do what they think you want them to do. So teaching them phrases like, 'I'm sorry, I don't know' or 'I don't understand' helps their development, their language, and their ability to communicate meaningfully in the classroom and elsewhere. Children in the older age group have developed beyond this stage in their own language, but need the expressions in the foreign language.

Here are some phases which all your pupils should learn as soon as possible. Note that they should be taught as phrases, not as words or structures. Children are only interested in what the phrases are used for. Some are very specific, most can be used in lots of different situations, and most give children a short cut to being able to function in the foreign language classroom.

Good morning/afternoon

Goodbye

Can I ...., please?

Sorry, I don't know/don't understand/can't.

What's this called in English?/What's the English for ....?

Whose turn is it/book is this/chair is this?

Whose turn is it to ....?

It's my/your/his/her turn.

Pass the ...., please.

Do remember 'please' and 'thank you' – they help a lot. So do the words for all the things in the classroom. Have picture dictionaries to help the children with the more common words. We have included a list at the end of the chapter of some of the picture dictionaries we are familiar with.

From Brian Abbs'
*Longman Picture
Workbook* (Longman
1987)

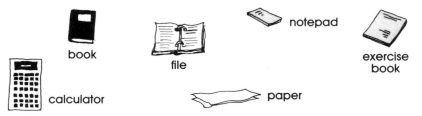

Try to speak English as much of the time as you can, using mime, acting, puppets and any other means you can think of to get your meaning across – see the section on presentation on pages 34 to 36. Your pupils are unlikely to have the opportunity to hear English all day so you should let them hear as much as possible while you have them in class. Keep your language simple but natural, and keep it at their level.

You will have to decide for yourself how much mother tongue language you use – it depends very largely on your own individual class. Remember that you can very often convey the meaning of what you are saying by your tone of voice and your body language – you don't always have to switch languages.

Questions and activities

1 Think back to when you went to school and try to think about the teachers you liked best. Why did you like them? Try to make two lists under the headings **Abilities** and **Attitudes.** Do the same with the teachers you didn't like. If you are working with others, compare your lists.

2 What abilities do you have that will help you in your teaching? Can you play a musical instrument, sing, tell stories, etc.? Is there anything you would like to be able to do that is not on your list? Can you do anything about it?

3 Read through the section 'Helping the children to feel secure' on pages 10 and 11. Make two lists under the headings:

> **Do** and **Don't**
> plan lessons   give pupils English names

Discuss your lists with a colleague if you can. Would you like to make any changes to the lists or add to them?

4 Make a list of tasks which pupils can do in your classroom, like changing the calendar.

5 Look back at the section on arranging the desks on pages 13 and 14. How would you like to arrange the desks in your classroom? Sketch a plan, leaving room for an English corner if you can. If you are thinking of a particular class, you can add the names of your pupils as well.

6 Let's say that you have a class of ten-year-old beginners. Which classroom phrases would you like them to be able to use at the end of the first two weeks? If you are using a textbook, look at the first lessons there and see what classroom language you think would be useful for these lessons.

References

Donaldson, M 1978 *Children's Minds* Collins
Underwood, M 1987 *Effective Class Management* Longman
Wright, A 1984 *1000 Pictures for Teachers to Copy* Collins

Picture dictionaries for general use in your classroom:

Abbs, B 1987 *The Longman Picture Workbook* Longman
Burridge, S 1985 *Start with Words and Pictures* Oxford
University Press
Crowther, R 1978 *The Most Amazing Hide and Seek Alphabet
Book* Kestrel
Eastman, P D 1964 *The Cat in the Hat Beginner Book
Dictionary* Collins and Harvill
Endeavour Picture Dictionary 1979 The Jacaranda Press,
Australia
Hill, L A and Innes, C 1981 *Oxford Children's Picture
Dictionary* Oxford University Press
Longman Elementary Dictionary 1987 Longman (Good for ten
year olds upwards)
Nelson, A and Hale, S 1979 *The Oxford Picture Word Book*
Oxford University Press
Parnwell, E C 1988 *The New Oxford English Picture Dictionary*
Oxford University Press (American English)
Rosenthal, M and Freeman, D 1987 *Longman Photo Dictionary*
Longman
Wagner Schimpff, J 1982 *Open Sesame Picture Dictionary*
Oxford University Press (American English)
Wright, A 1985 *Collins Picture Dictionary for Young Learners*
Collins ELT

3 Listening

Nobody spends a whole lesson listening, and we are not suggesting that any of the skills are taught or learned in isolation. The division into the four skills as chapter headings is simply a convenient and systematic way of presenting the teaching ideas in this book. What we are talking about in this chapter are activities which concentrate on the listening skill.

Listening in the classroom

These faces are copied from Andrew Wright's *Visual Materials for the Language Teacher*.

- It is quite clear that listening is the skill that children acquire first, especially if they have not yet learnt to read. When the pupils start to learn a foreign language, it is going in mainly through their ears and what the pupils hear is their main source of the language. Of course, we also give them as much visual back-up as possible through facial expression, through movement, through mime and through pictures.

- It is worth remembering too that once something has been said, then it disappears. If you're reading, you can go back and check, or you can re-read something you don't quite understand. This isn't possible when you are listening, so when we are talking and the children are listening, it's important to say things clearly, and to repeat them. When you are telling a story, for example, you don't have to tell it from beginning to end without breaks. You can re-tell it again and again as you go along:

  'This story starts on a nice, sunny Monday morning. Who's the story about? Who can we see in the picture? Yes, Fred and Sue. It's a nice, sunny Monday morning and Sue and Fred are . . . . Where are they? In the forest. Right. They're in the forest. And what are they doing? They're picking berries. So, it's a nice, sunny Monday morning, and Fred and Sue are in the forest picking berries. What happens next? Well . . . .' and so the story continues.

- Because the listeners can't re-listen in the same way that they can re-read, it means that if you are the listener, you can't decide how fast you work. Therefore, you have to concentrate very hard when you're listening. Young learners have a very short attention span. This is something which increases with age for most pupils, and you'll find that the eight to ten year olds can sit still and listen for longer periods. But it's important not to overload children when you're working on listening tasks.

- When we are talking to somebody who is saying something in everyday life, we usually understand what is being said and we say so – we nod, or we comment, or we show in some way that we know what the other person is saying. If we don't understand, then we usually say so at once. We very seldom wait until the end of a conversation or a story or an announcement and then start answering questions about what we have heard. The activities presented in this chapter try to ask for understanding as the children listen and not check for understanding only at the end of the exercise.

- Some listening activities will wake your pupils up, make them move about, create movement and/or noise. Others will calm them down, make them concentrate on what is in front of them, and create a peaceful atmosphere. Sometimes you want to have a nice quiet atmosphere and sometimes you want your children to move about, and you can use listening activities for both purposes.

'Listen and do' activities

Instructions

The most obvious 'listen and do' activity which we can and should make use of from the moment we start the English lessons is giving genuine instructions. Most classroom language is a type of 'listen and do' activity. Communication is two-way, and you can see very easily if your pupils have understood the message or not.

"Sit down, please."
"Come out to the board, please."
"Give this to Sylvie, please."

Moving about

There are also lots of 'listen and do' exercises which you can do with your children where they have to physically move about. The younger your pupils, the more physical activities they need. Children need exercise and movement, and you should make use of this wherever possible. As well as the moving about activities connected to doing ordinary things in the classroom, you can ask pupils to do all sorts of crazy things – 'stand on your head by the door' : 'hop on your left foot five times' – and the more language the pupils learn, the more you can ask them to do – 'count up to ten and then walk to the blackboard and back'. The advantage with this type of activity is that you know at once if the children have understood. You can check classroom vocabulary, movement words, counting, spelling, etc. Pupils learn from each other. If they haven't understood the first time, they'll still be able to do the activity by watching the others. As pupils learn more and more language, you can let them take over the role of 'instructor' – they are very good at it!

Put up your hand

You will almost certainly have to make use of the 'put up your hand' type exercise at some stage. For example, when the pupils are learning the sound system, you might ask them to put up their hands when they hear the sound /dʒ/. Or you might want them to put up their hands when they hear a certain word. Or, in order to calm them down a bit, whisper the numbers from one to twenty, and ask them to put up their hands when you miss out a number. There are all sorts of uses for the 'put up your hand when' type of exercise. Can you think of others?

Mime stories

In a mime story the teacher tells the story and the pupils and the teacher do the actions. It again provides physical movement and gives the teacher a chance to play along with the pupils.

Here's a very simple example of a mime story:

'We're sitting in a boat, a small rowing boat. Let's row. We row and row. Now what's that? A bird. A big bird flying over the water. Now it's gone. We keep rowing. Can we see the bird? No, no bird. This is hard work. Row, row. We're tired. We row slowly. There's the shore. Let's go home now. We're so tired we're dragging our feet. We're tired. We want to go to sleep. We lie down on our beds. We close our eyes, and . . . . shhhh . . . . we're asleep'.

Drawing

'Listen and draw' is a favourite type of listening activity in almost all classes, but remember that drawing takes time, so

keep the pictures simple. In 'listen and draw' activities the teacher, or one of the pupils, tells the other pupils what to draw. You can make up a picture or describe a picture you have in front of you. This activity is particularly useful for checking object vocabulary, prepositions, colours and numbers. It is not so useful for actions, since drawing people doing things is quite difficult for most of us.

Listening for information

'Listening for information' is really an umbrella heading which covers a very wide range of listening activities, and which could have been the title of this chapter. However, we are taking it to mean listening for detail, for specific information. These activities are often used to check what the pupils know, but they can also be used to give new information.

Identifying exercises

You can make up very simple identifying exercises like this one:

> "Has anyone seen this boy? He has dark hair and big ears. He is wearing rubber boots and carrying a football. He has a striped jersey and short trousers. Put a cross by the right picture."

This example is from Margaret Bautz's *Better English in the Classroom*.

Listen for the mistake

You can use the picture in your book but make mistakes in the text you read, so that pupils have to listen for the mistakes. The same can be done using the correct text and the wrong picture, but this takes a bit more time to prepare.

Putting things in order

Pupils have a number of pictures which illustrate a text in front of them. The pictures are not in the right order. Pupils listen to the text and put the pictures in the order they think is right. An example of this type of picture series is given on page 45 in the chapter on oral work.

Questionnaires

You can have a questionnaire type exercise which involves a little bit of writing or the filling in of numbers like this one, which is about how much television pupils watch:

Name	How many evenings?	How many hours each evening?	Total number of hours a week.
RICHARD	5	2	10
JANE			
THOMAS			
SUSAN			
PAMELA			
GEORGE			

This example is from *Are You Listening?* by Wendy Scott.

Questionnaires are a very useful type of language exercise which we have taken up again in the chapter on oral work. See pages 47 and 48.

Listen and colour

Children love colouring pictures and we can easily make this activity into a listening activity. We can use any picture which the pupils have in their workbook. Instead of just letting them colour it by themselves, make it into a language activity. Here is one which combines numbers and colours:

2 COLOUR BY NUMBERS ✏

Which colour?

1	....	white
2	....	brown
3	....	red
4	....	yellow
5	....	green
6	....	black
7	....	grey
8	....	blue

Tapescript:
The girl's trousers are brown, and she's wearing a yellow sweater. Her little boy has a white sweater and green trousers. The man reading the newspaper has a grey suit on, a blue tie and a black hat.
What colour is 6?

This example is from *Are You Listening?* by Wendy Scott.

Filling in missing information

Pupils can fill in the missing words of a song or a text or a timetable, like this one:

36 TIM'S TIMETABLE

	1st lesson	2nd lesson	3rd lesson	4th lesson	5th lesson	6th lesson
Monday	Nature Study					
Tuesday			P.E.	Reading	← Swimming →	
Wednesday			← Woodwork →		Music	Nature Study
Thursday	P.E.				← Games →	
Friday		← Cookery →			← Art →	

(LUNCH column separates 3rd and 4th lessons)

The tape tells the pupils about Tim's school timetable, and they fill in the missing subjects on their worksheets.

This example is from *Are You Listening?* by Wendy Scott.

For a discussion on using both textbook texts and authentic material for listening, take a look at Penny Ur's *Teaching Listening Comprehension*. It has lots of suggestions suitable for older children.

There are many, many different types of exercises which could be mentioned here. It is worth remembering that pupils are very good at making up this kind of exercise themselves. Getting pupils in one group to make up a listening task for the rest of the class or the members of another group is an excellent language activity. Make full use of the tape recorder and any other visual aids which you have available.

'Listen and repeat' activities

'Listen and repeat' exercises are great fun and give the pupils the chance to get a feel for the language: the sounds, the stress and rhythm and the intonation. When done in combination with movements or with objects or pictures, this type of activity also helps to establish the link between words and meaning.

Rhymes

All children love rhymes and like to repeat them again and again. Here you can use either traditional rhymes or modern rhymes, and you really don't have to worry too much about the grading. Rhymes are repetitive, they have natural rhythm and they have an element of fun, of playing with the language. Children play with language in their mother tongue, so this is a familiar part of their world, and it has an important part to play in their learning process. How about these two for a rainy day?

These examples are from Collins *English Nursery Rhymes for Young Learners*.

Rain on the green grass,
   And rain on the tree,
Rain on the house-top,
   But not on me.

Rain, rain go away,
Come again another day.
Little Johnny wants to play.

And this one about the dentist from Carolyn Graham's *Jazz Chants for Children* (Oxford University Press 1979):

I love coffee.
I love tea.
I hate the dentist
and the dentist hates me.

I love coffee,
I love tea,
I hate the rain
and the rain
hates me.

This last one and lots of others in the same book lend themselves to playing with language – the type of playing with language which we mentioned on page 5. What would you like to put in there instead of 'dentist'? Our words were 'housework' and 'rain'.

Songs

Songs are also a form of 'listen and repeat', and there are lots of books on the market with songs for children. We've included one or two of them in the booklist on page 32.

Exercises

The most obvious 'listen and repeat' exercises are the ones where the teacher or one of the pupils says something and the others repeat what has been said – it may be a drill, it may be words with special sounds, it may be a short dialogue using puppets or toy figures, or it may be a message to give to someone else.

Listening to stories

Listening to stories should be part of growing up for every child. Time and time again educationalists and psychologists have shown that stories have a vital role to play in the child's development, and, not least, in the development of language.

Make sure the children get the maximum benefit out of listening to stories in English by the creation of a friendly and secure atmosphere. Establish a story-telling routine which creates an atmosphere. Rearrange the seating so that you have eye contact – if you can, all sit together. Many teachers have their younger pupils sitting on the floor. It's important that children are comfortable. They don't have to sit up straight when they're listening to a story. If they're relaxed and comfortable, then they are more open to what they are about to hear, and they will benefit far more from the story-telling. You yourself might have a story-telling position. You might even have a beanbag chair to sit on. If you have the lights on in the classroom, turn at least some of them off.

"......So the farmer went and got his daughter, and his daughter held on to his son, and his son held on to his wife, and his wife held on to him, and they all pulled and pulled and pulled, but the turnip wouldn't move ...."

Listening to stories allows children to form their own inner pictures. They have no problems with animals and objects which talk – they can identify with them, and the stories can help them to come to terms with their own feelings. The teacher should not moralise or explain the story, although, of course, discussion is very important.

The structure of stories helps children when they come to telling and writing their own stories. Many stories are full of repetition in themselves, like the Turnip Story. Almost all stories are worth telling again and again. Stories also exclude all kinds of teacher talk.

Telling stories

We have made a difference between telling stories and reading stories. We'll look at telling stories first. If you tell a story, then you don't have a book in front of you. Telling stories to children of all levels means that you can adapt the language to their level, you can go back and repeat, you can put in all sorts of gestures and facial expressions, and you can keep eye contact most of the time.

Traditional fairy tales

Traditional fairy tales, like *Little Red Riding Hood* and *Goldilocks* make wonderful stories for telling. They have a clear structure, with a special type of beginning, middle and end. Any five year old will be able to tell you what is a proper fairy story and what isn't, even if they can't tell you why. They start off with a setting – when and where. The story is told in episodes – events which have consequences. One set of consequences leads to another event. There are goodies and baddies, and the goodies win. Most fairy tales have good story lines and you can either tell traditional stories from your own country or tales from other countries.

If you are going to tell traditional stories, then it is best that you go through the story first and write it down in sequence. For example, *Little Red Riding Hood*:

Setting: In a wood. Her grandmother's cottage.

Episodes: Little Red Riding Hood makes a lunch basket.
She says goodbye to her mother.
She skips and sings on the way.
She meets a wolf.
etc.

To see how fairy tales can be simplified have a look at *Favourite Fairy Tales* – a Longman series for young readers.

This will make it easier for you to remember the story as you tell it.

(Traditional fairy tales can, of course, be read aloud as well if you have a version which is simple enough.)

Creating stories

Another exciting form of story telling which you can do from a very early stage is to create stories with the children, so that you tell their story. First, the setting : 'When did the story happen?' 'Once upon a time' – you must accept the first answer that comes, no censoring allowed. 'Okay. Once upon a time in . . .?' 'Egg.' 'Fine. Once upon a time in a country, town called Egg. . . .?' 'Town' 'Right. Once upon a time in a town called Egg, there was . . .?' And so on. This gives a real feeling of a shared story and you cannot tell how the story will end – but it does, usually rather unconventionally. Making up stories with the children at all stages helps them to put their thoughts into words, and gives them a starting point for their own writing. We come back to the creating of stories in the chapter on writing.

Reading stories

Instead of telling a story, you can read aloud from a book. This is not the same as telling a story and in this case you should not change the story at all. Children like to have their favourite stories repeated, and they will very often be able to tell you the story word for word – they do not like changes being made. If children like learning stories off by heart, let them. There is sometimes a very narrow dividing line between learning a story off by heart and being able to read it.

Children of all ages love to be read to, and you should try to spend as much time as possible reading to the eight to ten year olds as well as to the younger group. For the older group it is often good to have a continuing story so that you read a bit of the book every time you see them.

Independent listening

We talked in Chapter 2 about having an English corner where you have a comfortable place to sit, books to read, a notice board, etc. If at all possible, you should also have cassettes here too, so that the children can sit and listen in peace and quiet. There is a lot of English cassette material available both for young learners of English as a mother tongue, and for foreign language learners. These are usually cassettes which come along with books, like the Professor Boffin books in the Longman *Easy Readers* series, and there is no reason why pupils shouldn't listen and follow the pictures before they can read the words. Young children need to have some sort of introduction to this type of material, and five to seven year olds in general should have listened to it first in class or with their group and the teacher.

Don't forget that sometimes we just want pupils to listen for the sake of listening – music and poetry or a short anecdote or story all have a role to play in the classroom. Try to introduce as many different voices into the classroom as you can, and remember that pupils need to hear many varieties of language. The more they hear, the better they will be able to speak and write.

Questions and activities

1 Look back at the mime story on page 23. Underline the words which you would act out in this story.
2 Can you write another short mime story? If you are working with other teachers, you might like to tell them a mime story at their level.
3 Can you remember a favourite story from your childhood? Think about it now. Try to divide it up into sections as we started doing with *Little Red Riding Hood* on page 29. Find a key word for each section so that you can remember it, then tell it to an audience.
4 Can you think of a fairy story in your own language which you think would be appropriate to tell six year olds? What about ten year olds? Take one of these stories and practise telling it in English and then tell it to an audience.
5 Record yourself reading a story, and listen carefully to the result. See if there is any way in which you could improve your reading.
6 Look through all the activities in this chapter again. List them under the headings **Quiet activities** and **Noisy activities.**

References

Bautz, M 1984 *Better English in the Classroom* NKS Forlaget, Oslo

Collins English Nursery Rhymes for Young Learners 1986 Collins ELT.

The *Favourite Fairy Tales* series 1988 Longman

Graham, C 1979 *Jazz Chants for Children* Oxford University Press, New York

The *Professor Boffin* readers in the Longman *Easy Reader* series

Scott, W 1980 *Are You Listening?* Oxford University Press

Ur, P 1984 *Teaching Listening Comprehension* Cambridge University Press.

Wright, A 1976 *Visual Materials for the Language Teacher* Longman

Song books

Abbs, B 1980 *Jigsaw First Songbook, Jigsaw Second Songbook*, and *Jigsaw Songbook*, Mary Glasgow Publications

Blyton, C 1972 *Bananas in Pyjamas, a book of nonsense with words and music* Faber & Faber

Byrne, J and Waugh, A 1982 *Jingle Bells & Other Songs* Oxford University Press

Case, D, Milne, J and Klein, M *Singlish* BBC English by Radio and Television

Dakin, J 1968 *Songs and Rhymes for the Teaching of English* Longman

My English Songbook 1981 University of York/Macmillan Press

Oral work

General comments

Limitations

Speaking is perhaps the most demanding skill for the teacher to teach. In their own language children are able to express emotions, communicate intentions and reactions, explore the language and make fun of it, so they expect to be able to do the same in English. Part of the magic of teaching young children a foreign language is their unspoken assumption that the foreign language is just another way of expressing what they want to express, but there are limitations because of their lack of actual language.

We don't know what they *want* to say

If you want your pupils to continue thinking about English simply as a means of communication, then you cannot expect to be able to predict what language the children will use. Their choice is infinite, and we cannot decide what they will say or want to say. You'll also find that the children will often naturally insert their native language when they can't find the words in English.

Finding the balance

What is important with beginners is finding the balance between providing language through controlled and guided activities and at the same time letting them enjoy natural talk. Most of our pupils have little opportunity to practise speaking English outside the classroom and so need lots of practice when they are in class.

Correction

When the pupils are working with controlled and guided activities, we want them to produce correct language. If they make mistakes at this stage then they should be corrected at once. During this type of activity the pupils are using teacher or textbook language, and the pupils are only imitating or giving an alternative, so correction is straightforward.

However, when pupils are working on free oral activities we are trying to get them to say what they want to say, to express themselves and their own personalities. The language framework of the activity is often quite tightly controlled by the teacher or the textbook, but the emphasis for the pupils should be on content. If pupils are doing problem solving or working on any of the activities of the types given on pages 42 to 48, then correction of language mistakes should not be done while the activity is going on. The teacher can note what he or she thinks should be corrected and take it up in class later. Of course, if pupils ask you what is correct or what the English word for 'X' is while they are talking, then you should give them the answer.

Presenting new language orally

When children start learning English, they obviously need to be given language before they can produce it themselves. Language has to go in before it can come out. At this initial stage the activities will be under the control of the teacher. Here are just some of the ways you can present new language orally:

Through the pupils

The teacher knows what his or her pupils can do, so he or she says: 'Listen to me, please. Maria can swim. Peter can sing. Miriam can ride a bike. Paula can whistle. Carlos can draw.'
The sentences should be true and accompanied by the appropriate actions and sounds.

Using a mascot

One of the most successful ways of presenting language to young children is through puppets or a class mascot. Having 'someone' familiar constantly on hand with whom you can have conversations about anything and everything is a wonderful way of introducing new subjects and new language to young children. For example, if you use a teddy as your mascot, you can use Teddy to ask questions. Pupils can ask through Teddy : 'Teddy wants to know . . .' You can present dialogues with Teddy as your partner.

For example:

'Teddy, can you swim?
No I can't, but I can sing.'
And Teddy then sings a song.
OR
'Teddy, do you like carrots?
Ugh, no!
What about bananas?
Yes I love them.'

Once the teacher has given the model, pupils can ask Teddy all sorts of questions and Teddy can provide all sorts of answers. In this way Teddy's name, address, identity, likes, dislikes, etc. will be built up in cooperation with the children, so that Teddy belongs to everyone in the class. Note that a mascot should belong to only one class. (See page 108 for other suggestions for a class mascot.)

Teddy means that you don't have to present oral work by yourself. Most oral work is directed towards someone and asks for a response from someone, and having another speaker of English around can make all sorts of situations easier to get across.

Drawings

You can use very simple line drawings on the board, like these from Andrew Wright's book *Visual Materials for the Language Teacher* (Longman 1976):

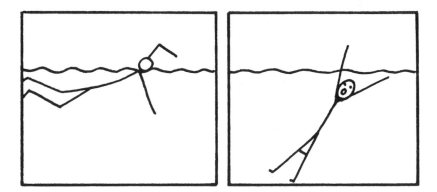

Silhouettes

You can use silhouettes on the overhead projector; they can be given movement if you attach a piece of wire to them. (another of Andrew Wright's ideas):

Puppets

Puppets don't need to be more than masks, and these don't have to be complicated. They can just be paper bags with holes for eyes:

Other suggestions

You can use simple and clear pictures to present new language; you can mime/act situations; you can use realia – clothes, telephones, animals, toy furniture, etc. What else could you use to present language orally?

Controlled practice

Controlled practice goes hand in hand with presentation since it is important that pupils try out new language as soon as they have heard it. In controlled practice there is very little chance that the pupils can make a mistake. In the Teddy example above, we have already suggested the controlled practice – that the pupils ask Teddy, 'Do you like ......?' They can then go on to ask each other in pairs, 'Do you like ......?', with the other pupil simply answering 'yes' or 'no'. Once the pattern is established with the class, they can happily do it in pairs. Again too, you can use the same variety of ways of getting the controlled practice going – Teddy, puppets, drawings, etc.

Here are two examples of controlled practice:

Telling the time

Pupil A asks: What's the time? Pupil B answers: It's ....

One o'clock   Half past seven   A quarter to two

What's he/she doing?

Pupil A asks: What's he/she doing? Pupil B answers: He's/she's ....ing.

This example is from D H Howe's *English Today!* Book 2

a.   b.   c.   d.

Activities like these provide the basis for oral work, but do not always produce 'real' language at once. Their purpose is to train pupils to use correct, simple, useful language within a situation or context. Pupils may have to repeat sentences, be corrected and go through the same thing several times. Familiarity and safety are necessary to help build up security in the language.

Guided practice

Guided practice follows on directly from controlled practice and will often be done either in pairs or in small groups. Guided practice usually gives the pupils some sort of choice, but the choice of language is limited. Textbooks are full of exercises for guided practice and you can use pictures or objects or miming to help the pupils understand the content and practise the words – telling the time, asking the way, talking about colours, etc. Here are a couple of such situations:

What's the time?

This exercise would follow on from the controlled practice above. Both pupils have clocks with hands that move. The situation could be that Pupil A's watch has stopped and he or she wants to ask Pupil B the time. This puts the language into context and the guided practice can become a mini-dialogue.
Pupil A : What's the time, please?
Pupil B : It's five past ten. (Looking at the clock in the book and putting his or her clock to five past ten)
Pupil A : Thank you. (Puts his or her clock to the same time and compares)
The language remains the same, but Pupil A never knows what the time is going to be. Since Pupil A has to do something with the information he or she gets, it also makes the exercise just a bit more meaningful.

Chain work

Chain work uses picture cards or word cards. Put all the cards face down in a pile. Pupil 1 picks up a card on which there are some bananas. Turning to Pupil 2 he or she says 'Do you like bananas?' Pupil 2 then picks up the next card on which there are some apples and answers, 'No, I don't like bananas, but I like apples.' Pupil 2 turns to Pupil 3 and says, 'Do you like apples?' to which Pupil 3 replies, 'No, I don't like apples, but I like. . . .' and so on. Obviously, this activity can be used to practise whatever vocabulary or structure you are working on at the time – it is not limited to bananas and apples.

Dialogues and role play work

Working with dialogues is a useful way to bridge the gap between guided practice and freer activities. Controlled dialogues can easily develop into freer work when the pupils are ready for it. Putting pupils into pairs for doing the dialogues is a simple way of organising even large classes.

First the teacher will have to present the dialogue in whatever way seems most suitable. You might like to use puppets, or Teddy, or a magnet board or a flannel board – it really depends on what you have available. Dialogues which involve some sort of action or movement are the ones which work best with young children. Intonation is terribly important too, and children love to play around with this. After the pupils have heard the dialogue a couple of times, and you've done it with some individuals, with you 'giving' them their parts, let them all repeat it with you, making sure that it doesn't become a chant. Then let half the class do it with the other half of the class and then let the pupils do it in twos.

Using objects

Here are two dialogues which show how physical movements or objects can make a dialogue come alive for young children, and give it an amusing communicative purpose. The day before, ask the children to have something unusual in their pockets the next day. During a quiet time, make sure that each one knows what the word for his or her object is in English.
The children can choose which dialogue they want to follow, and they can go through one or both with as many other pupils as you have time for.

– What have you got in your pocket?   – I'm not telling you.   – Oh, please?   – O.K. It's a frog.

– What have you got in your pocket?   – I'm not telling you.   – Then don't!

Clearly, there is a lot more involved in these exchanges than language alone, and you may find that you want to act them out in the mother tongue first. There are also endless ways in which these dialogues could develop, and young children will very quickly go outside the limits of what is set for them. This type of activity works well with the five to seven year olds as well as the older children.

Role play

Another way of presenting dialogues is through role play. In role play the pupils are pretending to be someone else like the teacher, or a shop assistant, or one of their parents, etc. For young children you should go from the structured to the more open type of activity.

1 Beginners of all ages can start on role play dialogues by learning a simple one off by heart and then acting it out in pairs. With the five to seven year olds you can give them a model first by acting out the dialogue with Teddy, and getting the pupils to repeat the sentences after you. With the older children you can act it out with one of the cleverer pupils.

A: Good morning. Can I help you?
B: Yes, please. I'd like an ice cream.
A: Here you are.
B: How much is that?
A: 45p. Thank you.
B: Goodbye.
A: Goodbye.

2 The next stage can be to practise the above dialogue, but asking for different things. Your class now knows the dialogue, and together you can suggest other things to ask for – a bar of chocolate, a bottle of lemonade, a packet of crisps. The prices will, of course, have to be changed too. If you are introducing 'a bar of, a bottle of, a bag of' for the first time, you might want to put the suggestions on the board, but otherwise you don't need to. Make it clear that when they are working on their own in pairs, they can ask for things which have not been mentioned, and they can add comments if they want to.

3 In real role play, the language used comes from the pupils themselves, so your pupils will have to be familiar with the

language needed before you can do the role play itself with them. This type of role play is more suitable for the eight to ten year olds at level two. The roles which the children play can be given to them orally, but if the children can read, then it is easier to give them written cue cards:

Customer	Shop assistant
You go into a kiosk to buy something for Saturday evening. Here are some of the things you can ask for: a bar of chocolate a packet of crisps a bottle of lemonade Remember to be polite.	You work in kiosk. A customer comes in. Here are the prices of some of the things you sell: a bar of chocolate 50p a packet of crisps 40p a bottle of lemonade 60p Remember to be polite. You start the conversation.

Again, those who want to can keep to the information given. Others might want to move into a freer activity and have a completely different conversation. Most pupils like to add a bit extra to rather matter-of-fact situations like this, and we have had customers grumbling about prices, the shop assistant trying to sell crisps that are old, lemonade which is the wrong colour, etc.

Dialogues and role play are useful oral activities because:

1 Pupils speak in the first and second person. Texts are often in the third person.
2 Pupils learn to ask as well as answer.
3 They learn to use short complete bits of language and to respond appropriately.
4 They don't just use words, but also all the other parts of speaking a language – tone of voice, stress, intonation, facial expressions, etc.
5 They can be used to encourage natural 'chat' in the classroom, making up dialogues about the little things which have happened and which occupy the children at that moment. At first these conversations will be a bit one-sided, perhaps taking place between the teacher and Teddy in the very beginning. But if the atmosphere in the classroom is relaxed and nobody worries too much about formal mistakes

or using the mother tongue now and then, then even beginners can have great fun trying out the little language they know. There is a very narrow dividing line between guided activities about things which you want to talk about and actually talking about them.

Free activities

Using controlled and guided activities which have choices wherever possible provides a good background for activities where children say what they want to say. Let's look first at some characteristics of free activities.

- They focus attention on the message/content and not on the language as such, although the language will usually be limited by the activity itself.
- There is genuine communication even though the situations are sometimes artificial. In a way, everything we do in the classroom is artificial – we do it to prepare pupils for their lives outside the classroom. But free activities are one step nearer real life – and they let us know that we can communicate in the foreign language.
- Free activities will really show that pupils can or cannot use the language – this is something which you cannot be sure of if you only do guided activities.
- Free activities concentrate on meaning more than on correctness. Formal mistakes don't really matter too much unless it means your pupils can't be understood, so, as we said in Chapter 1, leave correction until afterwards. In free activities we're trying to get the pupils to use the language with a natural flow – with what is called *fluency* – and so fluency is more important than *accuracy* at this stage.
- Teacher control is minimal during the activity, but the teacher must be sure that the pupils have enough language to do the task.
- The atmosphere should be informal and non-competitive. All pupils 'win'.
- There is often a game element in the activity.

Suggestions for mini-talks:
My room
My favourite meal
My pet
A good day
Saturday at home
My family
Pocket money

The range of free activities is endless and goes from playing card games to giving mini-talks or presenting personal or school news in English to working out what your partner had for breakfast. We have chosen to look at just a few of these activities which we know work well in classes of young children.

Most of them are based on the information gap principle – that A knows something B doesn't know, and B wants that information.

Pairwork

First let's look at some pairwork activities. Remember that quite a lot of pairwork activities can be done very simply in class by making half the class turn their backs to the teacher/overhead projector/blackboard, and making sure that all the pupils who have their backs to you have partners who are facing you. In that way, you can give information to the half of the class facing you, and they then have to pass it on to those who cannot see the teacher/overhead projector/blackboard.

1 With older children working in pairs, give one pupil map A and the other map B. Pupil A explains to Pupil B where the various places are, or Pupil B can ask where the places are. This is a restricted free exercise in that the vocabulary and language structures are limited, but that's how it should be. Don't give pupils exercises which are so free that they don't know where to start or can't cope linguistically.

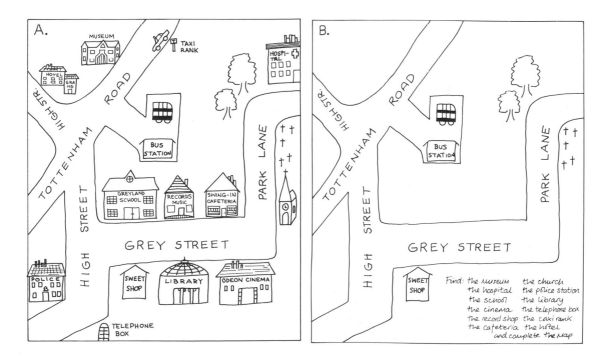

2 Here's an activity commonly used with younger children, but made a bit more communicative in the language sense by adding the information gap principle. Give everyone in the class a picture to colour – use one in your workbook. We've used a boy and a girl. Ask all the As in the class to colour the girl and all the Bs to colour the boy. Walk around and encourage them to talk to you about what they're doing. When they've finished, put an A with a B facing each other and ask them to ask the other person how they've coloured in their part of the picture: 'What colour is his shirt?''What colour is her blouse?' etc. It's important that they don't show each other or the point disappears. (They can stand a book up between them.) When they've finished, they should end up with two identical pictures. If they don't, then there's something wrong with their colour or clothes vocabulary! Note here that although the language limits are decided by the picture, the pupils still decide for themselves which colours they are going to use.

This drawing is from Wendy Scott's *Are You Listening?* Hong Kong Edition

In both these activities the teacher plays a non-dominant role – that of the organiser. The same is true for all these sorts of activities, whether pupils are matching cards, playing Happy Families, describing a picture for other pupils or doing a 'find the differences' activity in pairs:

 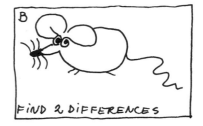

Groupwork

There are lots of examples of groupwork throughout this book, but here are two which are easy to arrange, fun to do, quite easy to organise and which concentrate on oral work.

1 Take any picture story from your textbook or workbook, copy it, cut it up and give one picture to each member of the group.

This example is from the *Longman Picture Dictionary*

Each pupil then has to describe to the others what is in his or her picture without showing it to the others. When the pupils have heard what is in all the pictures, the group decides on the correct order of the pictures.

2 Another story-telling exercise which needs a bit more imagination and is most suitable for the eight to ten year olds at level two is where everyone in the group has two objects or pictures of objects which have to be woven into a story. You can use your own objects or you can ask pupils to bring them along or decide beforehand what their two objects will be. You start off the story – 'I met a family yesterday who had never been in Hong Kong before. They were visiting

my neighbours.' The story then continues with one pupil adding to the story using his or her object, which might be a packet of tea, or a toy car, or whatever: 'Of course, they had tea with me' or 'I went out in the car with them' or whatever sentence comes out. As the story continues, it gets funnier and more ridiculous, and pupils have to help each other in the end to work their word into the story. This can also be done as a class story.

Whole class activities

In these activities all the pupils get up and walk about. Inevitably, they tend to be a bit noisy, and if you have more than thirty pupils in your class, you should split them into smaller groups.

1 The first activity is a matching activity. Make cards which are similar, but a little bit different.

Make two copies of each (if you want to make the activity more complicated, make several copies of each). Each pupil has one card, which they look at, memorise, and leave face down on the desk. Everyone then walks around trying to find the person with the identical card just by talking to each other. When they think they have the same cards, they check by looking at their cards, and then sit down at their places. If you have more than two copies of each card, then the activity will continue until all the matching cards have been found. This kind of activity is useful for prepositions, colours, actions and all sorts of object vocabulary.

2 Another activity which is useful and versatile and which we have already touched on in the listening chapter is using questionnaires. These are a mixture of groupwork and whole class work, as well as a mixture of written work and oral work. They can be guided or free activities. Split the class up into groups – the size will depend on how many pupils are in your whole class – and give them each a different task. Ask them to find out about favourite foods, favourite books, favourite television programmes, how much television people watch, when bedtime is, how much pocket money they get or whatever is relevant to what you are working on at the time. With the five to seven year olds you will have to provide the questionnaire, which might look something like this:

Which day do you like best?

name	Monday	Tuesday	Wednesday	Thursday	Friday	Saturday	Sunday
Salim				✓			

The eight to ten year olds should be able to work out their own questionnaire, although they will probably need help to work out the actual questions to ask to find out the information they want, and they will have to write them down. Again their questionnaire may end up being simple, just like the one above, or it may be quite complex if you have level two pupils. This one was used to find out who watched the most television, boys or girls, and if boys watched different types of programmes from girls.

a) Detective
b) Pop
c) News
d) Sport
e) Films
f) Series
g) Children's T.V.
h) Others

Name	Boy/Girl	Week days	Weekends	Type
Suda	B	2 hours	2 hours	b

Once the preparatory written work is done, they can all go around asking each other their own questions. They can present their results orally or in writing. Again, this is a structured activity but it involves communication and doing something with the information they're told. It can also involve a little bit of arithmetic and the setting up of tables.

Questions and activities

1 Look back at the exercise at the bottom of page 38. It uses cards which are all about food. Can you think of more topics you could make cards for?
2 Look at your textbook and list the activities from one lesson which are designed to practise oral language. Do you like them? Do you think they will be useful for your class? If you're not happy with them, how would you make them more suitable for your class?
3 Either on your own or with a colleague, add some more free oral activities to the ones given in this chapter. They may be things you've done in class or read about elsewhere, or they may be activities which you've thought out yourself.

References

Howe, D H 1985 *English Today!* – a 6-1evel course for children, Oxford University Press
Scott, W 1983 *Are You Listening?* Hong Kong Edition, Oxford University Press
Worall, A and Abbs, B 1988 *Longman Picture Wordbook* Activity Book, Longman
Wright, A 1976 *Visual Materials for the Language Teacher* Longman

Reading

Just as listening is the main source of language when pupils start to learn a language, print is the second main source. As pupils become better and better in the foreign language, the printed word becomes the main source of expanding and strengthening the language. Reading is also the language skill which is easiest to keep up – many of us can still read in a foreign language that we used to be able to speak as well. Books open up other worlds to young children, and making reading an enjoyable activity is a very important part of the language learning experience.

Approaches to reading

Many five to ten year olds are in the process of learning to read in their own language. Whether or not they have mastered the skill in their own language, and whether or not their own language is written in the Roman alphabet, will have an effect on the initial stages of teaching reading in English. For example, a German child of nine will already be familiar with most of the techniques of reading – with word divisions, sentence links, paragraphs, how letters relate to sounds, how the illustrations help him or her understand what is going on. A Japanese child of nine will also be aware of much the same things, but he or she may not be very familiar with the Roman alphabet or relate sounds to individual Roman letters. Clearly, children whose mother tongue is not based on the Roman script have more stages to go through when they are learning to read in English.

There are a number of different ways to approach the introduction of reading in a foreign language.

1 Phonics

This approach is based on letters and sounds. Basically, we teach the pupils the letters of the alphabet, and the combination of letters, phonically – as they are actually pronounced – so that the letter a is pronounced /æ/, the letter b is pronounced /b/, c is pronounced /k/, ph is pronounced /f/ and so on. It is best to start off with three or four letters that can make up a number of words, like c a n t. You can then show pupils how to pronounce /kæn/, /kæt/, /kænt/ and /tæn/.

Although phonics can become very complicated as all the pronunciation rules are introduced, it can be a very useful way into reading for those learners who are not familiar with the Roman alphabet or who do not have a one to one relationship between letters and sounds in their own written language. It is not to be recommended as the main way into reading for those pupils who are already reading in their own language using the Roman alphabet, and it should not be taught to pupils who are learning to read using phonics in their own language – this could lead to great confusion in pronunciation.

2 Look and say

This approach is based on words and phrases, and makes a lot of use of flashcards – words written on cards like this:

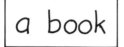 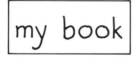

It is usual to start by teaching everyday words which are already familiar to the children. The teacher shows the children the word and says it while pointing to the object. The children repeat the word. This happens several times with each word. The introduction of the words only takes a short time, and goes quite quickly, so the teacher may spend five minutes of a thirty minute lesson on four new words. There are a lot of word recognition games which can be done at this stage – matching words and pictures, pointing to the object on the card, guessing which card Teddy has picked out of the hat – and so this approach encourages recognition of a range of words and phrases before 'reading' a text.

3 Whole sentence reading

Here the teacher teaches recognition of whole phrases and sentences which have meaning in themselves. This often means a story which the children read for the first time themselves after the whole text is familiar to them. The words are not presented in isolation, but as whole phrases or sentences. Since we think that reading for meaning should be encouraged as soon as possible, we will look at this approach in more detail below.

4 Language experience approach

This approach to reading is based on the child's spoken language. The teacher writes down a sentence for the child to read which is based on what the child has said. For example:

This is me.

My sister is nine. She is in class 3F.

This is a postcard from my uncle in Milan.

Again, since we think that this is a good, pupil-centred approach to reading, we will go into it in more detail below.

Which method to choose?

Clearly, if there was one correct method for teaching all children to read, then only one method would exist. We favour an approach which concentrates on meaning from the beginning. However, if your pupils have a mother tongue which is not based on the Roman script, you will probably find that you will have to spend quite some time teaching phonics and word recognition first.

No matter which approach to reading you take as your basic approach, you should remember that all these approaches are a way in to reading and are not an end in themselves. You will probably want to make use of all the methods described at some stage in the process of learning to read.

Five to seven year olds

- Five to seven years olds are likely to take longer to learn to read in a foreign language than eight to ten year olds. Some children starting school are not familiar with books or what they are used for. They have to go through the process of doing reading-like activities first – 'reading' from left to right, turning the pages at the right place, going back and reading the same pages again, etc. Picture books with and without text are invaluable at this stage.
- If your pupils have not learnt to read in their own language, many will not yet have understood what a word is, nor what the connection is between the spoken and the written word.

- Sentence structure, paragraphing, grammar – none of this means anything to most pupils at this stage.
- Decoding reading – making sense of what we see on the page – is a very involved process, and adults make use of all sorts of clues on the written page – punctuation, paragraphing, use of special words, references to things which have happened, hints as to what can happen. What five to seven year olds have instead is often a visual clue and this clue is vital to meaning.

Take, for example, *Belinda's Story* by Margaret Iggulden, a story written for four to seven year olds. The story is about an elephant called Belinda who goes around looking at animals of different colours. The text of the last three pages of the story is:

I'm an elephant and I'm grey.
That's an elephant. It's super.
I'm an elephant and I'm super.

Without the drawings, you don't know that the elephant is unhappy about being grey. Here are the last three pages taken from the book, with the accompanying illustrations:

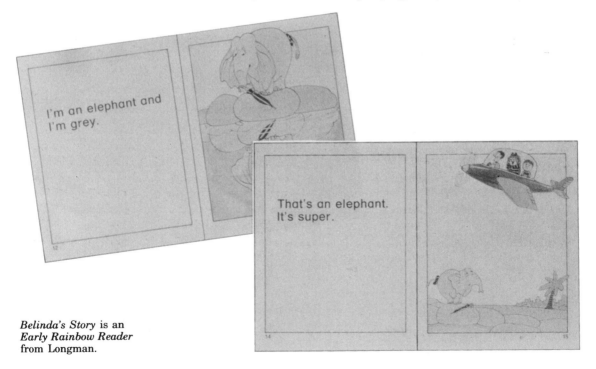

Belinda's Story is an
Early Rainbow Reader
from Longman.

I'm an elephant and
I'm super.

16

One of the conclusions to be drawn from this is that the illustrations in a book for young children matter almost as much as the words themselves.

Eight- to ten-year-old beginners

The majority of eight to ten year olds will already be able to read a bit in their own language and most seem to have little difficulty in transferring their reading skills to English. This means that you can spend much less time teaching the mechanics of reading, and concentrate more on the content. Children whose mother tongue is not based on the Roman alphabet will still have to spend more time on the mechanics of reading, but they know what reading is about, and this speeds up the process.

Starting off

Let us take as our example a class of six year olds who have English for three short lessons a week. Let's look at four possible starting points.

1 Reading a story from a book

Look back at what we said in Chapter 3 about reading stories. Some of the stories which you read aloud will become the stories that your pupils read. Let's take *Belinda's Story* as our example. The whole text of the story is as follows:

That's a bird. It's green.
That's a butterfly. It's red.
That's a fish. It's blue.
That's a crab. It's yellow.
That's a cat. It's white.
I'm an elephant and I'm grey.
That's an elephant. It's super.
I'm an elephant and I'm super.

a) Look back at what we said on page 28 about creating a routine for story reading. This is not a big book, so you will have to read with quite a small group.

b) Read the book so that all the pupils can see it, and point to the words as you say them. This is important if your pupils are to understand the connection between the spoken and the written word. It also helps these beginners to understand what a word is. Some children may think that 'butterfly' is two words. Read at just under normal speed the first time, keeping your intonation correct.

c) Let pupils point and ask questions if they want to, but not so much that it interrupts the flow of the story.

d) Encourage the pupils to talk about the story. Ask them questions in their own language, like, 'Why was Belinda unhappy?' 'Were the other animals unhappy?' 'Which animal did you like best?' 'Do you think Belinda is super?'

e) Leave the book in the book corner. Tell the group they can read it on their own if they want to.

f) The next week, read the story again. Let them give you some of the words.

> Teacher: 'That's a . . . .'
> Pupils: 'Cat.'
> Teacher: 'It's . . . . .'
> Pupils: 'White'.
> Teacher: 'Yes. That's a cat. It's white.'

g) Give all the pupils their own copy if possible and tell them to follow it while you read to them. Encourage them to point to the words as you read, but don't slow down.

h) If you see pupils pointing to the wrong words, sit with them and point with them.

i) Let them read the book silently for themselves.

j) Tell them they can read the book whenever they have time. Go back to it from time to time and read it with the whole class. Pupils don't usually get tired of good stories, and this is a good, simple story.

2 Reading a class story

Instead of reading from a book, you might want to use a class story as your starting point for reading. This has the advantage that you can photocopy freely, making sure that everyone has a copy, and the pupils can colour their own copies. There's also the point that shared stories are always a good starting point simply because they are shared.

In a class where Teddy is used, build up a short story about Teddy using the story-telling techniques already described in Chapter 3. If you have already read the story about Belinda, you and the pupils could make up a story about Teddy who doesn't like being brown/white/beige or whatever colour he is. This allows you to keep the same structure, but bring in more colours and animals:

That's a bird. It's orange. That's a fly. It's green. That's a frog. It's green too. That's a zebra. It's black and white. I'm Teddy and I'm beige. He's Teddy and we love him. He's great. I'm Teddy and I'm great.

When you make the book ask pupils to help you with the illustrations if they can. These ones were done by nine year olds at Mosstodloch Primary School in Morayshire.

Your story can now be treated in the same way as above, but you can give the pupils their copies quite quickly. Remember that Teddy's story must look like a book with pages to turn and pictures to look at.

3 Reading texts based on the child's language

This approach has proved effective with beginners in both age groups. The idea is that each individual pupil has his or her own written text which says what he or she wants it to say, and is used for both mother tongue and foreign language learning. When working in the foreign language, it is important that the teacher does not set the pupil a task which he or she does not have the words for in that language. For example, there's no point in pupils bringing in a picture of the place where they live, if they have no words to talk about it.

This type of reading is often based on a picture, but can be about something which has happened, or just about how the pupil is feeling today. It is easiest to start off with a picture.

a)   Ask the child to tell you about the picture.

b)   If he or she gets stuck, ask either/or questions. 'Is she tall or small?'

c)   If this still doesn't work, let the child tell you what he or she wants to say in his or her own language. If this translates into something familiar, talk about it, make sure the child understands. Do not write words which are new or unfamiliar.

d)   Write a sentence in the child's book based on what the child has told you. It can be very simple. 'This is me at home.'

e)   Let the child see you writing the sentence, and say the words as you write them.

f)   The child repeats the sentence after you, pointing to the words as he or she says them.

g)   This is now that pupil's reading task, which he or she can read aloud to you.

h)   It shouldn't take more than a couple of minutes to do this – you have a lot of pupils in your class.

i)   This sentence can gradually be built on. 'This is me at home. It's my bedroom. It's blue. It's nice. I have fish in my bedroom.'

j)   As the child's vocabulary increases, you can gradually build up stories.

The same technique can be used for making up group/class reading books. This technique of writing down what your pupils say or the stories they tell you helps the five to seven year olds to see that print is a means of communication, and that there is a relationship between the amount of talking that is done and the amount of writing on the page. For both age groups, it is important that the pupils see themselves as writers with something to say.

4 Reading familiar nursery rhymes or songs
Most children learn nursery rhymes in their mother tongue and in English without having a complete understanding of what they're saying. Some nursery rhymes are produced as books, so the children can 'read' what they already know off by heart. While you might say that this isn't real reading, the pupil can behave like a reader, and it helps to build up confidence. As we have said before, there is also a very narrow dividing line between knowing something off by heart and actually reading the words.

Reading aloud
Let us now move on to look at various reading techniques. When we went to school, most of the reading done in class was reading aloud. Reading aloud is not the same as reading silently. It is a separate skill and not one which most people have that much use for outside the classroom. But it can be useful, especially with beginners in a language.

Traditionally, reading aloud is often thought of as reading round the class one by one, and although many children seem to enjoy it, this type of reading aloud is not to be recommended:

- It gives little pleasure and is of little interest to the listeners.
- It encourages stumbling and mistakes in tone, emphasis and expression.
- It may be harmful to the silent reading techniques of the other pupils.
- It is a very inefficient way to use your lesson time.

However, reading aloud is a useful technique when used slightly differently:

- Reading aloud to the teacher should be done individually or in small groups. The reader then has the teacher's full attention. Reading aloud from a book lets the teacher ask about meaning, what the pupils think of the book, how they are getting on with it, as well as smooth out any language difficulties which arise. High priority should be given to this kind of reading aloud, especially at the beginner stage for all ages. By the time pupils progress to level two, this kind of reading is not so necessary.

- The teacher can use it as a means of training and checking rhythm and pronunciation. The teacher can read a sentence or a phrase and the class or parts of the class can read in chorus after. This is particularly useful if the text is a dialogue, but should only be done for a very short time. Choral reading can easily become a chant if there are a lot of children in the class.

- Reading dialogues aloud in pairs or groups is an efficient way of checking work. The pupils can help each other with words they find difficult to pronounce, and you should try to get them to be a little critical about what they sound like: 'You don't sound very friendly, Michelle' or 'Are you angry, Heinz?'

The following reading text is clearly suitable for reading aloud, and gives lots of opportunity for reading with expression:

This example is from *Snap!* Stage 1.

- Listening to a pupil reading aloud should be a treat for the whole class. If pupils are going to read aloud for the rest of the class, they must be well prepared and the others should want to hear what is going to be read.
  'Maria is going to read you a story she's written with me. It's about a princess and a bird.'
  'Peter has written about his trip on board his uncle's boat and he wants to read it to you.'

Silent reading

Reading aloud can be a useful skill to have in the classroom, and one which teachers make good use of, but silent reading is what remains with most people for the rest of their lives. Nobody can guarantee that all your pupils will love books, but a positive attitude to books and reading from the beginning will help. Make as much use of your English corner as possible (see page 12): have print everywhere, put up jokes on the notice board, give your pupils messages in writing, try to give them their own books, even if it is only a sheet of paper folded over to make four pages, make books available to them, and listen to what they are saying about their reading. Use the textbook to concentrate on conscious language development, but let your pupils read books for understanding and for pleasure.

Building up confidence

- Some children are natural readers and will want to read books as soon as they can, but you should spend some time building up confidence with the whole class about silent reading. Give them all a story that they have listened to before and give them, say, two minutes to see how far they get. Talk about the story with them in the mother tongue after they've read it. Clear up any difficulties. The emphasis is on the content and the language shouldn't be a stumbling block. Let them finish the story at their leisure.
- Give pupils only half the story, and discuss what happens next in the mother tongue. See how many different endings are possible, then let them read the rest of the story to see if they were right. From the beginning encourage this type of anticipating. Good stories put the reader in the mood of wanting to know what happens next.
- For the eight to ten year olds who are beyond the beginner

level, you might want to use silent reading as the starting point for role play for the whole class or for a smaller group. If the book is written in dialogue form, then they may want to act some of it out for the rest of the class. If the book is a story, then the pupils will have to work out their own roles and what they say.

Different reading materials

Once your pupils are on the road to reading, it is important that there is as wide an individual choice of reading materials available to them as possible.

Reading cards

You may want to start off with reading cards in a box or a book pocket.

It is very simple to make a collection of reading cards which tell a story and can be read quickly. A one-page story still gives a sense of achievement. You might have different stories with the same characters either from the textbook you're using or characters which your pupils have invented during class story time. Some of the reading cards can have nursery rhymes on them, but try to choose the easier ones. Here are two examples of reading cards adapted from primary textbooks:

Treasure
Text from *Sam on Channel 9*, Stage 2. Illustration Jorgen Ytreberg.

Sheila's rabbits
Text and illustration from *Up To You* i Plus.

You may want to add questions on the back of the card. These may be questions about the story in the child's first language to begin with, but in English later.

Home-made books

These may be different verses of a song the children are already familiar with. Or they may be class stories written down by you. In addition to teacher-made materials, you also have pupil-made books, which are an essential part of any class reading corner/library.

Books for native speakers of the language

Children with English as their mother tongue are learning to read at the same time as your pupils and so there is a wide choice of books available. This is particularly true if your pupils start early. If your pupils start learning English at ten, then you should make sure that the books at their level of language are not too childish.

Easy readers for foreign language learners

Most of the major publishing companies publish series of easy readers. Many are aimed at the adult market, but there are more and more series for younger learners. The age range and the word level is often specified in the publisher's catalogue. We have included a list of some of these series at the end of the chapter.

Picture dictionaries

To begin with, pupils can just look at picture dictionaries in the same way as they look at picture books. Later on, they will learn to use them to find words, check spelling, expand their vocabulary, etc. There is a list of picture dictionaries on page 20.

Books with tapes

Some books for native speakers of English and some easy reader series have accompanying tapes. These can provide useful listening and reading material both for slow readers and for those who progress quickly. However, you should encourage pupils to try reading without the tape as well. Some pupils become lazy readers if they listen to too many 'speaking books', and stop trying to become real readers.

Introducing new books

There are different ways of introducing new books to the pupils. Ideally, at the five to seven stage you should read all new books to the whole class, but there isn't usually time for this. However, a new book should not just appear. You can:

a) show the pupils the new book and tell them what it's about.

b) look at the cover of the book and try to work out with the pupils what it might be about.

c) read them an amusing or interesting bit from one of the books.

Suddenly they heard a little
    boy's voice:
"But the Emperor isn't
    wearing any clothes!"
"Don't be stupid!" the boy's
    father said.
"But he hasn't got any
    clothes on," the boy said.
"The boy's right," a woman
    said.
"Yes, he's right!" a man
    said. "The Emperor
    hasn't got any clothes on."

From *The Emperor's
New Clothes* in the
Longman *Favourite
Fairy Tales* series.

d) put the title of the new book on the notice board.

A new book for you to read

This is the cover of *The Nose Book* in the *Beginning Beginner Books* series.

Book reviews

It is always a good idea to find out what pupils thought of a book, even if they stopped half way through. Book reviews

a) help you to decide on the suitability of a book,
b) give you some indication as to the progress the pupil is making,
c) help other pupils to decide about the book,
d) help pupils to develop a critical approach to reading matter and
e) show that you are concerned about what your pupils are reading.

As pupils become older and more critical you can encourage them to write 'real' book reviews, but you can start off very simply, like this:

DINO THE DINOSAUR	🙂	😐	🙁
PUPILS' NAMES			
MARIA N.		✕	
PETER	✕		

Questions and activities

1 Which of the ways of teaching reading are familiar to you? Were you taught to read using one of them? How are pupils taught to read their own language in your country?

2 Look back at the section on reading aloud on pages 57 to 60. Can you think of times other than those mentioned here when it would be useful for your pupils to read aloud either to you, the teacher, or to other pupils?

3 We've mentioned a number of ways of introducing new books to the pupils. Which do you think would be the most effective? Can you think of any other ways of introducing new books?

References

Ekman, L, Peterson, L and Soderlund, K, 1982, *Up To You* Plus Book 1, Aschehoug, Norway

Iggulden, M 1986 *Belinda's Story* Longman

The Emperor's New Clothes 1986 Longman

Perkins, A 1970 *The Nose Book* Random House, New York

Webster, D and Cobb, D 1983 *Sam on Channel 9*, Stage 2 Longman

Series of readers

This is only a very short and completely personal selection of readers which are suitable for children. The series of easy readers from the major English Language Teaching publishers have not been included here.

Beginning Beginner Books and *Beginner Books*, Collins and Harvill

Breakthrough to Literacy Longman for the Schools Council

Dunn, O *Ranger Story Workbooks* Macmillan

Favourite Fairy Tales 1989 Longman

Groves, P *Bangers and Mash* Longman (concentrates on the sounds of the language)

Howe, D 1983 *Start with English readers* Oxford University Press

Ladybird books. This series is written for native speakers and covers a wide range of subjects.

Starters Macdonald Educational (covers Places, People, Maths, Activities, Long Ago, Nature, Science and Legends)

Strange, D 1988 *Start Reading* Oxford University Press

Writing

We assume here that your pupils can already write in their own language or are in the process of learning to write. However, since the process is a long one, we also assume that most of your pupils will still be coping with the mechanics of writing as well as thinking about what to write.

Writing is not always easy

Although the writing and the oral skill are combined in the classroom and the one clearly benefits from the other, writing has certain characteristics which seem to make it difficult for pupils to get to grips with, especially for younger pupils:

- You can't make the same use of body language, intonation, tone, eye contact and all the other features which help you to convey meaning when you talk.
- Very little of what you write is concerned with the here and now, which is where many young children exist for a lot of the time. Exercises which reflect the pupil's world help to bridge this gap. A copying exercise could be: 'Carlo is very happy today. It is his birthday. He has got a kitten.' Or you might have a fill-in exercise about Teddy: 'Teddy has got a new .... We think it is very ....'
- Many children take a long time to master the skill of writing. In a survey done in Britain in 1982 on attitudes to writing in the mother tongue, about 10 per cent of eleven year olds thought they were being asked about the mechanical problems of writing – pens and pencils, neatness, etc. If the teacher can occasionally type out a pupil's work it really does help those who are struggling with the mechanics of writing.
- The last comment reflects the fact that writing in a foreign language is all too often associated with 'correcting errors'. Handwriting, grammar, spelling and punctuation are often given priority over content. If we try to make children's writing meaningful from the start, with the emphasis on

content, then errors can be gently corrected and re-written in cooperation with the teachers: 'This is the way you spell "like". Put "is" in front of "sitting" and then it's fine.'

Writing is a good thing

Even if there are difficulties in writing in the foreign language, it is still a useful, essential, integral and enjoyable part of the foreign language lesson.

- It adds another physical dimension to the learning process. Hands are added to eyes and ears.
- It lets pupils express their personalities. Even guided activities can include choices for the pupils, like the copying activity on page 70, or the story about the pet on page 73.
- Writing activities help to consolidate learning in the other skill areas. Balanced activities train the language and help aid memory. Practice in speaking freely helps when doing free writing activities. Reading helps pupils to see the 'rules' of writing, and helps build up their language choices.
- Particularly as pupils progress in the language, writing activities allow for conscious development of language. When we speak, we don't always need to use a large vocabulary because our meaning is often conveyed with the help of the situation. Lots of structures in the language appear more frequently in writing, and, perhaps most important of all, when we write we have the time to go back and think about what we have written.
- Writing is valuable in itself. There is a special feeling about seeing your work in print, and enormous satisfaction in having written something which you want to say. Never underestimate the value of making pupils' work public – with their consent, of course.

Controlled writing activities

Writing activities, like oral activities, go from being tightly controlled to being completely free. You will usually do more guided activities with beginners, but you should not exclude very simple free activities. In general, controlled and guided activities are being done to practise the language and concentration is on the language itself. Free activities should allow for self expression at however low a level, and content is what matters most.

Straight copying

Copying is a fairly obvious starting point for writing. It is an activity which gives the teacher the chance to reinforce language that has been presented orally or through reading. It is a good idea to ask pupils to read aloud quietly to themselves when they are copying the words because this helps them to see the connection between the written and the spoken word. The sound–symbol combination is quite complicated in English. For children who find even straight copying difficult, you can start them off by tracing words. Even though they may not understand what they are 'writing', they will still end up with a piece of written work, and this in itself will give valuable encouragement and satisfaction.

Matching

You can vary straight copying by asking pupils to match pictures and texts, or to choose which sentence they want to write about the text. For example, pupils might choose from the three possibilities about this picture:

Write *one* sentence:

- He likes cooking.
- He is a good cook.
- He is making a nice meal with eggs and onions.

Organising and copying

Copying can also be a good introduction to structured writing, as in this example:

Complete Kate's letter:

163 Palmetto Dunes
Miami
July 14th, 1984

Dear Michael,
    Miami is fantastic. ....
....
    Yesterday ....
....
    Tomorrow..
....
                                        Love, Kate

| we went to the cinema. | It's got beautiful beaches. |

There are a lot of hotels and restaurants.

Then we went to a restaurant.

we're going to visit the famous Aquarium.

| The water is green and warm. | We saw a very good film. |

This exercise is from the Activity Book which accompanies the *Snap!* series, Stage 2.

Delayed copying

You can do 'delayed' copying, which is fun to do in class, for training short term visual memory. Write a short, familiar sentence on the board, give the pupils a few seconds to look at it, and then rub it out and see if the pupils can write it down. Please note that this type of activity should not be used as a test.

Copying book

It is useful for pupils to have a copying book where they can copy new vocabulary, a little dialogue, something you want them to remember or whatever. Most pupils will keep to what you ask them to copy, but they should be free to copy things from the textbook, the notice board and from other pupils. Some pupils will copy whole stories. If they have the time to do it, let them.

Dictation

Dictation is a very safe type of exercise if you can keep the language elementary and simple, and because you, the teacher, are providing the actual language as well as the context. For young learners, dictations should

- be short
- be made up of sentences which can be said in one breath
- have a purpose, and be connected to work which has gone before or comes after
- be read or said at normal speed.

Here is a short, simple dictation which acts as a message to the class:

'Maria has a baker's hat. She's going to bring it to class tomorrow. We're going to have a baker's shop.'

Guided written activities

Fill-in exercises

Fill-in exercises are useful activities, especially at the beginner stages. They do not require much active production of language, since most of the language is given, but they do require understanding. With children who have progressed to level two, they can be used to focus on specific language items, like prepositions or question forms. Try to avoid exercises which have no meaning at all – exercises which give you sentences like 'The ox is on the bed.'

Fill-in exercises can be used for vocabulary work. For example, if the pupils are familiar with the words for pets and a few adjectives, then this text has meaning even though there is no picture to put it in a context.

My Pets

We have got three family pets: a ...., a cat and a tortoise. The dog's name is Big Ben. He is a .... golden Labrador. He is beautiful. He has got big .... eyes and a long tail. He is a very friendly dog, but he is sometimes a bit .... Dogs are expensive to keep, but they are very good guards for the house.

Dictation

You might like to try dictating only half a sentence, and asking pupils to complete it in their own way. For example,

I like ....

I don't like...

I hate ....

I love ....

You can either ask pupils to complete each sentence before you read the beginning of the next sentence, which encourages quick writing, or you can give them time to do the completion afterwards. This type of exercise is a good starting point for discussion in the pre-writing stage of free writing. This one could be used as the starting point for a bit of free writing on 'What I like doing best.' See pages 75 to 77 for a fuller discussion of pre-writing activities.

Letters/cards/invitations

Letter writing seems to be a popular language class activity, and it is indeed a useful way of getting pupils to write short meaningful pieces of writing. Ideally, letters are written to be sent, but you can have pupils writing to each other and 'sending' their letters via the classroom postman. Here is a very simple guided exercise which can be used quite early on:

Dear   ....,

Are you free on ....? .... going to the .... Would you like to come with ....?

Love   ....

And the reply:

> Dear ....,
>
> I'd love to go to the .... with .... on
> ....
>
> Thanks.
>
>   Love ....

or

> Dear ....,
>
> I'm sorry I can't go to the .... with .... on
> ....
>
> Thanks anyway.
>
>   Love ....

Free writing activities

- Above we looked at examples of activities designed to develop
  the pupils' writing, with most of the language being provided
  for them. Pupils then need to be able to try out their
  language in a freer way. In free activities the language is the
  pupils' own language, no matter what their level is. The
  teacher should be the initiator and helper, and, of course, is
  responsible for seeing that the task can be done by the pupils
  at that level. The more language the children have, the
  easier it is to work on free writing activities.
- What about correcting the pupils' free writing work? If it is
  possible, this should be done while the pupils are still
  working on it. The teacher should try to look at the work
  being done, perhaps at the rough copy stage, correct mistakes
  and suggest possible ideas, words, etc. Pupils should write in
  pencil and use a rubber. You do not always have to correct
  all the mistakes. The aim is to produce a piece of written
  work which is as correct as you can expect from that pupil.
  This means that you may be handing back work which is not
  completely correct. You may also display work which has
  mistakes in it – as long as the pupils are seeing lots of other
  written language this won't matter.

- Older pupils beyond the beginner level should be encouraged to re-write their work, so the final product is not what they hand in for correction, but the result of working on the piece of writing. The teacher should give as much help as possible to the pupils both before the actual writing task begins and while the writing is going on. Pupils usually want what they write to be good, and some will not mind writing their final version out nicely once they have mastered the mechanics of writing. But if your pupils are just learning to write or if they find writing difficult, then don't ask them to re-write. Like all other language activities, writing should be enjoyable.
- Although it can be expensive and it is not possible for all classes, ideally each pupil should have a folder or a ring binder of his or her own to keep all written work in. Pupils can decorate their own folders and learn to keep their work in order, perhaps by putting the date on everything they write. If everything a pupil has written is in one place, then both the teacher and the pupil can see how much progress is being made.

Pre-writing activities

The main difficulty with free writing activities seems to be going from nothing to something. Even pupils with lots of imagination don't always know what to write about. Their vocabulary is limited. They are still not confident about the mechanics of writing. All pupils need to spend time on pre-writing work – warm-up activities which are designed to give them language, ideas and encouragement before they settle down to the writing itself.

Talking about the subject

A short simple conversation about the subject can be enough to get ideas going and collect thoughts. With the five to seven year olds, you might start them off by simply asking a question : 'What did you do last night?' and writing some of the answers on the board : 'watched TV, played football, had supper, read a story', etc.

Word stars

First put the key word on the blackboard. You are going to
write about pets, so you decide to use *dog* as your key word.
Put the class into groups and ask them to write down all the
words they can think about connected with dogs. Often pupils
want to put in a word they don't know the English word for.
Just let them write it in their own language and you can fill it
in in English later. When all the groups have made their word
stars, you can do one on the blackboard for everyone. This gives
the whole class not only words, but also ideas about what to
write. This is the kind of result you get from six- to
seven-year-old beginners:

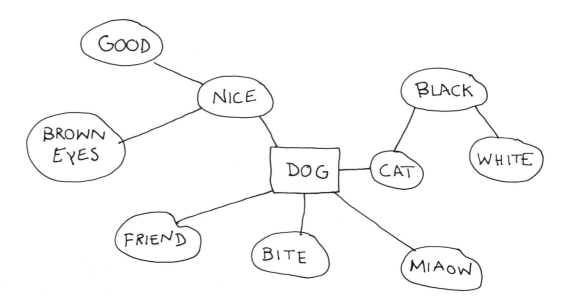

Vocabulary charts

Simple drawings or pictures with vocabulary collections are fun,
easy to make and always useful reminders of the words. Make
use of the idea of picture dictionaries here. The pupils might
like to make a picture dictionary of their own, using their own
themes and ideas. Pupils can try a sentence or two beside their
labelled drawings, too.

Here we have used a picture to collect vocabulary, but, of course, you can use a photograph, a story, a song, a piece of music or a shared experience for the same purpose. The aim is to give the pupils as many words and ideas as possible before they start on the actual writing task.

Topic vocabulary
Vocabulary can also be built up by collecting related words. See how many animal words you can get on the blackboard, for example. Say to pupils: 'Tell me two animals you like. Tell me two animals you don't like. What's the smallest animal you've seen? What's the biggest animal you've seen? Tell me two animals which we don't have in this country.' Of course, pupils will not know the names for all the animals. Use picture dictionaries as much as you can, but have your own dictionary too – you won't always know the words either. Pupils do not have to remember all these words – you are only collecting words to help them write their story.

We move on now to the writing activities themselves, and, as always, this section mentions only a limited selection of the range of possibilities.

Dialogues

Have a look again at what we said about using dialogues on pages 39 to 42. The dialogues the children write function as basic communication at all levels if they are spoken before they are written and used as reading texts after they have been written. The dialogues can be guided, following a very strict pattern, or they can be completely free. They can be very short and to the point, or they can be long and complicated. Best of all, perhaps, they can be about any topic.

a) Speech bubbles can be very useful for both

simple dialogues: and **for setting the scene:**

b) The following dialogue is the result of pairwork based on a model dialogue, but it is clear from the type of language used that a lot of work has been done on spoken dialogues before this. These ten-year-old pupils have put in the repetitions which would be there automatically in spoken language if someone was trying to remember the information they were being given.

Brown: Excuse me can you tell
me the way to the
Library, please.
Miller yes Go, along North Road and
turn left.
Brown: yes. left,
Miller: and go along Green Street,
cross the Oak Street
Brown: cross the Oak Street yes.
Miller: and go along to the
Church Road and turn Rigth
and there is a big house
and that is the Libary

c) The dialogue below was also the result of pairwork, but this time working on a given situation. This dialogue was typed out by the teacher and used as a reading dialogue afterwards.

Jennifer and Steve meet in a little sweet shop. The lady behind the desk is asleep. Jennifer and Steve are whispering.
Steve: Hello, what is your name?
Jennifer: My name is Jennifer. What's your name?
Steve: My name is Steve. Why is the lady sleeping? Is she ill?
Jennifer: I don't know.
Steve: But I want to buy some sweets!
Jennifer: Are you very fond of sweets?
Steve: Yes. Let's go to another sweet shop.

Descriptions

Lots of free writing includes descriptions, as do dialogues, but straight picture description can become a bit dull – 'I can see a .... I can see five ....' etc. – unless you spend time doing preparatory work. We would suggest as a stage up from labelling and listing that you talk about a picture or a scene with the class. Suggest spin-offs, which can be as simple as 'I like jam', and encourage an imaginative approach by asking leading questions like: 'Do you like ....? Have you got ....? Have you eaten ....? Have you been ....?'

Collages

A collage is usually a large piece of paper or a board which is made into a poster or a picture by sticking on illustrations, texts and other materials. Here is one contribution to a written collage about Christmas:

Now it is Winter.
The school is over.
The christmas is coming
Nothing is Nicer than that.

Christmas was the theme, and a wintery picture was used as the starting point for discussion in class. After the discussion, which resulted in lots of winter and Christmas words being written on the blackboard, individual pupils wrote a short piece on what they thought about Christmas. These were then all put together in a Christmas collage, along with some winter drawings and photographs, cut-out snowflakes, and a woollen hat.

Picture descriptions

When you first prepare a piece of written work orally, then you must expect the language to reflect this. The description of an untidy room on the following page was written by two older pupils in their third year of learning English, and we can see the effect of oral work in the question at the end of the description. Clearly no correction or re-writing has been done as yet!

I can se two pair of trousers.
And there's two panties and a shorts.
There's many shoes: five and there's a pair
of wellingtons, too.
Can you see the gloves who's lying in front
of the smallest girl? And the vest who's
hanging in the lamp?
On the desk you might see some tights,
panties, stockings and a slip.
Maybe it was an idea to tidy up a
little bit?

Letters

Dear Mrs T.,
I am angry
today. Grrr!
Tomas

Dear Tomas,
why are you so angry?
Can you tell me?
Love, Mrs T.

As we have already said, a real letter should be written to someone. The first free letters could be little notes to other pupils along the lines of the guided letters on pages 73 and 74. They can also be written to the teacher, and these letters should be answered without any comments on the language. Some teachers like to have this type of correspondence with their pupils regularly, just to see how they are getting on. For pupils who are beyond the beginner level, this teacher–pupil correspondence, which is private, may take the form of a diary instead of a series of letters.

When the pupils can write longer letters, it is a great advantage if you can establish contact with an English-speaking class or a class in another country where they are also learning English as a foreign language. Letters to imaginary people are not nearly as interesting or as much fun as letters to real pen-friends. Class letters, cassettes and individual letters are all possible if you have contact of this kind.

Stories

If you have followed our advice in the previous three chapters about story telling, then your pupils should be prepared for writing their own stories. Writing group stories is a good idea since the actual writing can be shared, and re-writing is not such a burden. Make sure that pupils do lots of pre-writing activities so that they have something to write about and the words to express what they want to say. Give them as much help as possible as they go along. Remember that most pieces of writing are written to be read by others, so the final version should be on a reading card, in the form of a pupil-made booklet, on a teacher-typed card, or simply on a piece of paper which can be put on the wall of the classroom.

Free writing covers a much wider range of activities than we have gone into here – poems, book reviews, advertisements, jokes, postcards, messages etc. – anything which has length or substance. Writing is an exciting and rewarding activity and is the most visible of the skills. Becoming a writer in a foreign language is magic – pupils can take writing home; their writing can be displayed; they can look back in their folders and see how much better they can do things now. So take time to make their writing as good as possible.

Summary of dos and don'ts on free writing

Do

- concentrate first on content.
- spend a lot of time on pre-writing work.
- make sure that it springs naturally from other language work.
- try to make sense of whatever the pupils have written and say something positive about it.
- encourage, but don't insist on, re-writing.
- display the material whenever possible.
- keep all the pupils' writings.

Don't

- announce the subject out of the blue and expect pupils to be able to write about it.
- set an exercise as homework without any preparation.
- correct all the mistakes you can find.
- set work which is beyond the pupils' language capability.

Questions and activities

Sun/19/1./86.

Dear Auntie Wendy,
I got youre parcel
the Night Nichola and I
phoned you PLEASE keep this
paper as a souvinier, some-
-thing very lucky is I keep
meeting Nichola around the corner.
I'm feeling very exited for sunday
tea grub and for the story.
because the story goes on
for a long time on sunday Night.
Lots
of
love
x x x x x Alex x x x x

1 Have a look at this letter from an eight-year-old native speaker at boarding school in England.
  Clearly, he makes spelling mistakes and he isn't too good on sentences, paragraphs, sequencing, etc. But, he says what he wants to say and that's what we have to concentrate on to begin with. What facts does Alex tell his Auntie Wendy in the letter?
  By concentrating on *content*, we can see that the letter is quite a good piece of writing.

2 We talk in this chapter about the importance of doing warm-up exercises – pre-writing exercises. Take a quick look through the chapter on oral work and note down the activities in this chapter which could be used as warm-up activities.

3 We have mentioned just a few free writing activities. Make a list of them and then add your own suggestions. Look through the chapter on oral work and note down the activities in this chapter which could be used as warm-up

References

Pupils' Attitudes to Writing at Age 11 and 15 1987 Department of Education and Science (APU) NFER
Snap! An English Course for Younger Learners in 3 Stages 1984 Heinemann

7 Topic-based work

Some textbooks these days are topic-based. In other words, the emphasis of the lessons is on a subject, a topic or a theme, and the contents of the book are arranged around these topics. Other textbooks for young children are story-based or activity-based. If your textbook is not topic-based, it does not exclude doing work on a topic in class.

Why do topic-based work?

We are not suggesting that topic-based teaching is the only way to organise your teaching, but we would like to suggest that it is a useful, helpful, practical and exciting way to teach either all of the time or some of the time. Here are some of the reasons why:

- When you are concentrating on a particular topic, the content of the lessons automatically becomes more important than the language itself. This means that it is easier to relate the. lessons to the experiences and interests of your pupils.
- Working on topics can help the learning process. The children can associate words, functions, structures and situations with a particular topic. Association helps memory, and learning language in context clearly helps both understanding and memory.
- Topic-based teaching allows you to go into a subject in depth and brings out reactions and feelings in the pupils which are not always covered in the textbook. It follows from this that pupils will usually need more and/or different vocabulary than the textbook provides. This in turn brings the learner and the learner's needs more into focus.
- Working on topics allows you more easily to give a personal or local touch to materials which may not have been produced in your country. Lots of books, including this one, have a section on pets, but this topic will not be relevant if you live in a country where people don't have animals as pets. You

may want to change the topic to talk about animals in general. How you organise your material within a topic is very personal and is dependent on the particular class that you are teaching at that particular time.

- Topic-based teaching allows you to rearrange your material to suit what is happening generally at the time of teaching. It allows you to work across the curriculum in a way which structure-based or strictly textbook-based language teaching doesn't. If you are working in a school and the school works on cross-curricular topics or projects, then your English lessons and their content will have to fit in with the rest of the school.
- The amount of time that you spend on a topic can be as long or as short as you like, depending on how much interest it arouses, how much language work you think you're getting out of it, how much time you have available and how much material you have.
- Since the emphasis in topic-based work is on content, the work in the classroom naturally includes all the language skills as well as guided and free activities.

How to set about it

Choosing your topic

Usually the teacher will decide which topic to work on, but if the pupils are interested in a particular subject, and you think they can do it in English, then try to work it into your timetable. If you are working in an infant or primary school, have a look at what the pupils are doing in other classes. For example, if they are doing 'growing' in Nature Study, then you could do some of the activities in English – measuring and comparing, for example.

Planning time

- Ideally, you should decide at the long term planning stage which topics you are going to work on and how long you plan to spend on each topic (see pages 98 and 99). Sometimes topic work will simply crop up while you are working on the textbook – you may come across a text which the children are particularly interested in or enthusiastic about. In this case, you may only want to spend one or two lessons on the particular topic, and this would be decided almost on the spur of the moment.

- If you have not done topic-based teaching before, then it is probably best to start off on a very small scale. Taking just one lesson on a topic which the children are particularly interested in and which may or may not be based on the textbook will give you some idea of the possibilities which this kind of teaching opens up. For example, let's say that you have pupils in their second year of English, and the textbook is doing 'pets' and has some guided writing activities on these structures:

'Have you got a pet? Yes, I have. No, I haven't.
Has he/she got a pet? Yes, he/she has. No, he/she hasn't.
What pet has Anna got?'

You know that several of your pupils have got pets, and that they like animals. You have a budgie yourself. So, you can expand the guided written exercises like this:

Everyone tells the class about a pet they know. 'I've got a grey cat. Her name is Muppet.' or 'Akiko has a dog. He barks.'

Pupils write and/or illustrate what they have said. You can then make a collage by pasting all their contributions on a big piece of paper or putting them all on your notice board under the heading 'Pets'. Afterwards you can go back to your textbook and continue with the exercises there.

Collecting material

Once you have some idea of possible topics, you should start looking for materials at once – all sorts of written and spoken texts, pictures, objects, cards, ideas. When you find something, make a note of it at once. If you can write on the back of the material, do so, otherwise write it down on a piece of paper, label it and then put it into the ring binder or cardboard box you keep for that topic.

We always think we'll remember our brilliant ideas, but we don't unless we make a note of them.

Similarly, once you've finished with a topic, make sure that all the materials you used go back into the relevant files and boxes – even the material which didn't work well. Next year you may have a different use for it. The teacher will do most of the collecting and all the filing but the pupils can often help to find pictures and objects in connection with a particular topic.

Functions and situations

Once you have your topic and a collection of connected materials, work out which situations and functions of the language you want to concentrate on. If, then, 'pets' is your topic, and you want to spend two weeks on it, you might want to take up :

Playing with a pet	Asking parents for a pet
Visiting a pet shop	Zoos
Favourite pets	Feeding your pet, etc.

And useful functions of the language might be:

Describing	Asking for something
Expressing likes and dislikes	Future wishes

The point is that the topic decides which situations and functions you can take up, and you have to make a selection as to which ones you want to concentrate on. You may find this difficult, but when in doubt, choose your situation first. If you concentrate on the function, you may well lose sight of the content matter. Of course, pupils will cover a far wider range of language in their work, but it is useful to know what you want them to be able to do by the end of the topic period.

Methods and activities

Familiarity nurtures security, so make use of the full range of what is already familiar to the pupils as well as activities which are in the textbook. However, you may find that stepping outside the textbook can lead to much more creative thinking on the part of teachers and pupils alike. Topic-based work opens up all sorts of possibilities.

The temptation in doing topic-based teaching is to let the free activities take over, but remember that the input and the guided activities have to be there too, just as the simple activities have to be there alongside the more challenging ones.

Assessment

Since topic-based work is complete in itself, it gives you and the pupils a good opportunity to assess what you've been doing. Do this assessment in the mother tongue. Ask the children what they liked/didn't like doing. What they would have liked to spend more/less time on? Which stories did they like? Do they think another class would like the same topic? Ask them what they think they have learnt and use the opportunity to repeat what's been gone through in class: 'Yes, now you know how to ...., and you can talk about ...., and you know all about ....'

Although small children find this type of assessment very difficult to begin with, it is well worth starting in a very casual way with the five to seven year olds. Young pupils take tremendous pride in being taken seriously, and we could perhaps spend a little more time finding out and taking into consideration our pupils' reactions and opinions. For example, we could decide with the pupils what to display for the rest of the school or for a parents' evening.

Food: beginners

Let's look now at the type of materials which you could collect for two different topics. We've chosen to look at 'food' and 'friends'. Do remember that what you collect is entirely dependent on where you are, the situation you're in, your pupils and your school as well as the level of the class. You can easily do either of these topics very successfully without using any of the material which we suggest here. We've considered 'food' as a broad topic which might take about twelve lessons in all, but which should perhaps be done in two blocks of six lessons.

Materials:

Lots of pictures collected by yourself and the pupils
menus, lists of prices
actual food (on the day itself!), tins, packets of food etc.
cups, saucers, etc.
recipes
listening texts
stories about food
songs and rhymes

a cake
(keik)

chocolate
('tʃɔklət)

Situations and functions:

- We want our pupils to be able to describe local food as well as some 'foreign' foods they may be familiar with.
- We want them to be able to follow simple recipes, and give instructions on how to make simple dishes.
- We want them to be able to behave politely at table in English.
- We want them to be able to express likes and dislikes.
- We want them to be able to do simple shopping.

Structures they should know by the end of the topic period:

- I like/don't like ....
- Would you like ....? No, thank you/thanks. Yes, please.
- Can you pass the ...., please? Here you are.
- Imperative for giving instructions.
- First ...., then ...., then ....
- I've got .... Have you got ....?
- Can I have ...., please? I'd like ...., please.
- How much is it?

Having decided on what you want the pupils to learn, there are lots of ways of tackling the work itself. Here are just a few suggestions.

Vocabulary work

- Cards – pictures pasted on cardboard or bought cards – can be used to present the vocabulary, along with actual food which you can bring in or ask pupils to bring in on the day. While you're doing the presentation you can put in 'Do you like ....?' questions or 'Would you like ....?' questions, along with 'Do you have .... for breakfast?' 'Is there anything here you hate/love?' etc. How you present the material and the structures you use depends again on what you have decided to concentrate on.

- To practise the vocabulary, you can use card games, like Find Your Partner, or Memory or Food Dominoes, and make them to suit your topic:

You will find lots of examples of simple games in Shelagh Rixon's book *Fun and Games, Card Games in English for Juniors.*

- You can do listening comprehension work like this exercise where pupils have to place the right food in front of the right person as they listen. They cut out the different foods before they start to listen.

12 BREAKFAST

This example is from Wendy Scott's *Are You Listening?* Hong Kong edition.

Tapescript

Mrs Wong would like tea with milk and sugar and two boiled eggs.◆ Mr Wong would like coffee.◆ Both Mr and Mrs Wong like toast and butter.◆ Grandfather isn't very hungry, so he only wants a sandwich and a glass of orange juice.◆ Wing Yan would like noodles and some milk.

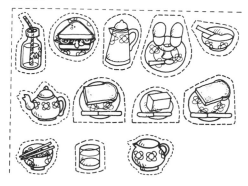

- If your pupils have a meal at school or bring packed lunches, make sure they can tell you all about them.

Dialogues and role play

- After vocabulary work you can move on to dialogue work and role play. Start off with dialogues like this very simple one (which can also be presented orally only):

This example comes from the Stage 2 Activity Book in the Heinemann *Snap!* series.

- Let pupils gradually move on to much freer work using cue cards. Alternatively, pupils can make up their own lists using their own pictures, or make up the most fantastic meals they like. Have a look at the progression in the role play presented on pages 40 to 42 in the chapter on oral work. If you have picture dictionaries in the classroom, then you will certainly find a section on food, which will be useful here.

Free activities

You can bring Teddy into the topic, and set the pupils to work in groups, with one group making up what Teddy would have for his birthday tea, another working on a teddy bear's picnic, another on what Teddy would serve if the headteacher came to tea, another on Teddy's favourite breakfast, etc. The completed work can be oral or written – a collage, a list, a dialogue, a play, even a story.

If you want to concentrate on shopping, then you can easily set up a shop in your English corner. Many teachers like to have a shop set up in the classroom all the time since there are so many uses for it in the first few years of language teaching.

Stories, songs and rhymes

You will find lots of rhymes in Julian Dakin's *Songs and Rhymes for the Teaching of English*.

In between doing all this you can have stories, songs and rhymes. Read them *The Hungry Caterpillar* or the Turnip Story (see page 28) or any other story you can find which you think is interesting and which is connected with your topic. There is an

Polly put the kettle on,
Polly put the kettle on,
Polly put the kettle on,
We'll all have tea.

Sukey take it off again,
Sukey take it off again,
Sukey take it off again,
They've all gone away.

enormous choice of songs and rhymes to do with food, like the following:

Hot Cross Buns
The Muffin Man
Fish, fish all in a dish
One potato, two potato
Pat a cake

Recipes and making food

For this part of the work, you will need to have the cooperation of the cookery teacher, or else choose recipes with no actual cooking involved, like making sandwiches or salad.

You can start pupils off by asking them about what they can make, if anything. This will be entirely dependent on where you live, but young children do enjoy being able to help in the kitchen, even if it's only cutting out the pastry.

Find recipes which will be relatively familiar to the pupils. Ask them what they think you do first: 'What do I need to have?' 'What do I do then?' 'And after that?' etc. Build up the recipe with them, then show it to them on the board or the overhead projector.

You might like to give them something new like this:

This recipe is from *Crown,* a Mary Glasgow Publications magazine for school children.

Of course, the climax of this lesson would be preparing the dish, and eating it, but please remember that there are all sorts of rules and regulations involving children and hot cookers, so you may want to get another teacher to do the actual cooking bit for you, or keep to recipes like the one above where there is no cooking involved.

Assessment

This will follow the general lines given in the paragraph on page 88, although in this case the children may think that the success of this topic work depends on whether or not they enjoyed 'Banana boats'!

Clearly, there are many other things which you can do with the topic 'food' – we have only given you a few suggestions. As we said in the beginning, one of the exciting things about working with topics is that you can adapt the topics to your own class, their interests and your own teaching style.

Friends: nine to ten year olds, level two

'Friends' is a topic which is quite likely to come up because of something in the textbook or an incident in class, and so we've dealt with 'friends' a bit differently. Two of your pupils may have been fighting. Some of your pupils may refuse to work with others. There may be best friends who refuse to be split up. In this case you may want to spend just two or three lessons on the topic, and you may not have that much material. What is important here is to get pupils to talk about being friends and what it involves, and that may be your only aim. You may not even specify a language aim. The emphasis here will be on pupil-produced work.

Making a topic like this work depends very much on the type of pupils you have and on the atmosphere in the classroom. Because of this, our suggestions are not so concrete or specific as they were for the topic 'food'.

Activities

What is a good friend?
Start the pupils off by talking about this in class, getting as many suggestions as possible. Ask them all to complete the sentence; 'A good friend ....' They can write as many sentences as they like. Each pupil reads one sentence to the

class. The sentences are collected to make a 'Good Friend Poster'.

What do you quarrel about?

Ask your pupils to close their eyes and think about the last time they quarrelled with a friend. Make a list on the board of all the things they quarrelled about. Ask them in groups to put the list into two columns 'Important things' and 'Unimportant things'. You can follow this up by setting up a situation with two characters and ask your pupils to make up 'quarrel dialogues'.

My secret friend

At the end of the first lesson on friends, ask all your pupils to write their names on a piece of paper. Put them in a box and ask each pupil to take one piece of paper. The person they pick is their secret friend for the next week, and they have to be extra kind and helpful towards that person. At the end of the week, each pupil has to guess who their secret friend was. If they can't guess, then the person in question has to say what he or she did to be specially kind and helpful.

The ideal friend?

Give pupils some examples from a quiz about friends:

These examples are taken from the Mary Glasgow magazine, *Clockwork:* No 4 1982–83.

Working with the pupils, find other situations involving friends and write them on the board. Then, using the above quiz as a model, pupils can make up their alternative answers in groups. You can either get the groups to try out the questions on each other or choose the best alternatives to each question and make a class questionnaire on 'My Ideal Friend'. This questionnaire can then be given to other classes to answer.

Questions and activities

1 Look back at the 'food' topic in this chapter. If you only had three lessons to spend doing food, which activities here would you do, and which would you leave out?

2 What local recipes could you use with five to seven year olds? Write them out in simple English.

3 Which topics are you particularly interested in? Could you use them with your class next term? If you have a textbook, look through it to find what subjects are covered there. Make a list of possible topics that *you* would like to do.

4 Take one of the topics which you listed above and think about it for five minutes. Note down all the ideas which come to mind. Look back at the way we organised the 'food' topic and try to organise your topic in the same way. Try to sketch out just two or three lessons.

5 Here is a short questionnaire for use with the eight to ten year olds at level two after they have been working on a topic for six lessons. Do you think it is a good questionnaire? If not, how would you change it?

TOPIC : HOBBIES

1. Did you have enough time to do what you planned?

2. Did the pupils in your group work well together?

3. Are you satisfied with the collage/sketch/booklet you made?

4 What did you learn from this period?

CLASS B. 4th year English

---

6 Look again at the questionnaire about 'The Ideal Friend' on page 94. Try to make up questions for 'The Ideal Pupil' and 'The Ideal Teacher', so that you could use them with the older children.

References

Carle, E 1970 *The Hungry Caterpillar* Hamish Hamilton

Crown a magazine for school children available from Mary Glasgow Publications, Ltd., 140 Kensington Church Street, London W8 4BN. The example used here comes from No 5 : 1984–85

Clockwork – another Mary Glasgow magazine for slightly more advanced learners, available from the same address as above.

Rixon, S 1983 *Fun and Games, Card Games in English for Juniors* Macmillan

Scott, W 1983 *Are You Listening*? Hong Kong Edition Oxford University Press

Snap! An English Course for Younger Learners 1984 Heinemann

Planning your work

Young children are usually full of enthusiasm and energy, and the language lessons will be full of variety and changes of activity. There is very little time available during a short lesson for you to actually *think*. So, as we said in Chapter 2, if you and your pupils are going to get the maximum enjoyment and the maximum learning out of a lesson, then the lesson must be carefully planned. All good teachers plan, just as all good teachers are prepared to adapt their plans, and know that they have to be prepared for emergencies.

Why good teachers plan their work

1 It makes life much easier for you in the classroom.
2 It saves time:
   - you can adapt the plan for future use.
   - you get quicker at preparing work with experience.
   - you become aware of how much time activities take.
   - it's much quicker to check at the end of a lesson what actually happened.
3 You know what you will need for each lesson.
4 You can more easily see how to balance your lessons.
5 As we said in Chapter 2, it gives you security and confidence, which is passed on to the pupils.
6 It allows you to use more of your energy and enthusiasm to enjoy what you're doing instead of worrying about what to do next, or looking at the next page of the book.
7 You can sometimes sit back and observe what's going on instead of planning the next activity in your head.
8 As pupils get older, they become more aware of how well-prepared the lessons are, and they like to have well-prepared lessons.

When, how and with whom to plan

We can divide planning into three stages:
- long term planning, which may be for a whole term,
- short term planning, which might be for a unit of work,
- and lesson planning for individual lessons.

Although long term planning is followed by short term planning, which is followed by lesson planning, the three types of planning are different.

Long term planning

- Long term planning will take place either before or at the beginning of term, and you can do it before you ever see your pupils. If you can, discuss with other teachers using the same book or series of books what they think about aims, methods and assessment.
- Talk to the parents about what you intend to cover if this is at all possible. If you are going to have the same pupils as last term, ask them what topics they are interested in. Give them a choice, and involve them at this stage if you can.
- If you are using a textbook, look through the list of contents and the teacher's guide. If the book is topic-based, you might decide to change the order, or to miss out something which isn't suitable for your pupils – you don't want to be talking about Father Christmas in the middle of June!
- If you are not using a textbook, decide roughly what you want to cover this term and how long it will take you for each unit/topic/language item.
- If you are working in a school where other subjects are taught, try to work with other subject teachers as well. For example, if you want to do a topic covering 'food' as outlined in Chapter 7, then this has to be put into the cookery teacher's long term plan too.
- If you are teaching in new surroundings, you should check where everything is and what there is at school. Things which are used in other subjects can be used in the English lesson too. Maps, for example, are always useful and can be borrowed from the geography teacher.

A term plan for the five- to seven-year-old group may look like this if you are teaching without a textbook:

SEPT.	OCT.	NOV.	DEC.
	The classroom. Colours	The body. What we look like.	School visited by foreign students.
			Food. Look, feel, taste
Me and my family	Outside school. Numbers.	Puppet work on preceding topics.	
			Decorate corridor outside Engl. room.

Or, it may look like this if you teach the eight to ten year olds and you're using *Sam on Channel 9*, Stage 2:

SEPT.	OCT.	NOV.	DEC.
	Your pets.	The Delta TV Studios.	What's Your Hobby?
		Camping.	
Sam on Channel 9.	Sam's diary.	Sam is ill.	Happy Christmas.
	The Delta Rally. NB! HALLOWEEN	Sam's horoscope.	

(Hallowe'en is not in the textbook)

Short term planning

- Once your long term planning is done, then the short term planning is much easier. You may be planning the lessons on one topic, the lessons for one unit in the book or the lessons for one week. A short term plan usually covers from three to ten lessons. If you have another teacher doing the same work at the same level, you can work together at this stage, although many teachers prefer to plan alone.

- If you are using a textbook, then much of the work at this stage is done for you. Most textbooks are written by experienced teachers and the lessons are carefully thought out. If you are new to teaching, then follow them as far as you can. The more you teach, the easier it gets to change other people's plans. After a time, you may find that you have different timing, different problems, and different classes from the ones your textbook is written for.

- Look at the texts which are in one unit in the book, or which you have collected. Note down if there is anything that you have to make or the children have to make.

- Decide what language items you are going to teach.

- Make quite sure *you* know how the language items are used. Perhaps you should look them up in a grammar book, just in case.

- Decide roughly on the way you want to teach the unit, and find activities that suit your topic.

- Assessment is part of teaching, so write assessment into your plan at this stage. Both teachers and pupils like to know how they're doing.

- Don't let your short term planning get too detailed. It is only a rough guide, but it should show clearly where you are going and what you hope to cover.

Here is an example of a teacher-made plan for a class of nine year olds:

Topic/Time	Texts & materials	Language items	Activities	Assessment
Food and drink. 2 weeks (6 lessons)	Magazine pict. Brochures Textbook texts Recipes Muffins? Songs Rhymes	Expressing likes and dislikes Phrases used during meals Food vocabulary Shopping lang., esp. questions (Can I have? Do you have? Would you like? How much is?)	Make shopping lists Pairwork interviews on favour. food Arrange classroom shops & use for shopping dial. Make posters/collages on daily meals Read food texts in ET mags.	Comment during less. Select with class 2 posters for exhibition school hall Informal ass.m. on content & efforts with class

Lesson planning

- Lesson planning has to be done before every lesson. Unless you work with another teacher in the classroom, you should do it alone. If you have done short term planning, then the lesson planning is easier – you know what's gone before and you know what's coming after.
- Most new teachers start off by writing very detailed plans, which become less detailed with time. This is not because teachers become lazy, but because planning becomes easier with practice and so experienced teachers don't have to note all the details.
- Here are some points to remember when making your lesson plans:
  1 Decide when and how to use group work. Make the organisation of your classroom as easy as possible – see Chapter 2.
  2 Link this lesson with the one before, and think about the one after.
  3 The time of day is important. Don't do long noisy exercises at four o'clock on Friday afternoon.
  4 Indicate how much time you think each activity will take.

5 Always have more activities than you think you will need.
6 Balance: quiet/noisy exercises
     different skills: listening/talking/reading/writing
     individual/pairwork/groupwork/whole class
      activities
     teacher–pupil/pupil–pupil activities

Here are two examples of teacher-made lesson plans:

Lesson plan: 5 year olds. 25 minutes. 1st lesson Tuesday.

Unit: Food and drink

Check overhead bulb!

Activities	Time	Materials
1. Register		
2. Repeat from Thursday 'One Potato Two Potatoes' in chorus twice.	5 min	
3. Present dialogue, two puppets: I like bananas (etc., countables!) So do I Here's one for you. Thanks!	5 min	Pictures (Bananas, apples, pears, potatoes, sweets etc.)
4. Chorus work on dialogue: full class all lines, then divided into 2 groups for statements and responses. Picture Cues. Then pairs	10 min	
5. Show drawing of children at party. Give some info' for listening, then "Tell me what you can see."	5 min	Drawing. Overhead (or pin to board)
6. Extra: "Pat a Cake"		

Lesson plan: 9 year olds. 40 minutes. 5th lesson Thursday.

Unit : Food and drink

Check text in green file. "Clockwork" from library.

Activities	Time	Materials
1. Sing "Polly Put the Kettle on" 2. Listen to story. How many "food words" do you hear (7)? Go through them.	10 min	Mrs G.'s story in the green file.
3. Repeat shopping dialogue for pupils. Then oral pair work. Pick grocer, baker, butcher and sweet shop owner for next lesson's shops (Maria, Peter, Les + Anna)	10 Min	Dialogue from Tuesday lesson.
4. Choice of reading or writing exercise: a) Multiple choice exercise from MGP Series 6 – "Table Manners" b) Write a shopping list for tea-party/dinner/birthday party.	10 Min (More?)	MGP mags.
5. Make flashcards for the 4 shops. Make sure all shops covered. May be extra exercise	10min (Less?)	List of foods for the shops on board. Crayons.

NB! Ask Maria to bring her baker's hat next lesson.

How did it go?

When you are looking at how your planning worked out, the most important question to ask yourself is, 'Did the pupils learn what I wanted them to learn?' This can be a difficult question to answer since learning takes place over a period of time, but a good time to ask the question is after a whole unit in the textbook or after a series of lessons on a topic.

When it comes to looking at individual lessons, not all teachers come out of a lesson and go through their lesson plan in detail. You don't have to. When you plan the next lesson you usually check how far you got, what you gave for homework, etc. If you don't do it after every lesson, you should sit down at the end of the week and go through your lesson plans, marking what you did and what you didn't do, and if the activities worked or didn't work. Don't spend too much time analysing each lesson. Go through it quickly and see what you can learn from it, then file it away for future reference.

You can make a quick checklist:
1 Did the pupils understand the teaching point? Did they learn what they were supposed to learn?
2 Did the organisation work?
3 Did they like the subject matter?
4 Did I do this part of the lesson?
5 Was it the right kind of activity at that stage?

What to do when things go wrong

Unless your pupils are angels, and you are a gifted teacher, you must be prepared for things to go wrong, or rather, not as you planned. Young children are wonderfully spontaneous, and do and say whatever comes into their heads. Their enthusiasm sometimes overflows. If they are interested in what they are doing they will show it. They cannot concentrate for long on one activity, and, of course, they will find other things to do if their concentration goes. Unless a child is actually being destructive, then try to make the 'bits that went wrong' into something positive. Sometimes the lesson where nothing goes as you planned can be very successful.

Several types of things can go wrong:

An external disturbance

Something is disturbing the class – a wasp is buzzing around the classroom, or a number of fire engines are passing the window. In cases like this, either get rid of the disturbance – kill the wasp or get it out of the room – or make use of it: 'Oh look at all those fire engines!' Teach the word 'fire engine' and then go back to your plan as quickly as you can.

An internal disturbance

Something is disturbing one or two of the class – perhaps one of the pupils bursts into tears, or two of them start fighting. Take the pupil(s) aside – you might want to take them out of the classroom. If the class is already working individually or in pairs, then you can simply tell the others to get on with what they are doing and hope that they do. If this happens in the middle of a class activity, give the pupils something quick and easy and quiet to do, like 'Think about/write three words beginning with *p*' or 'What was the best/most difficult new word last week?' Of course, once you've sorted the problem out, you then have to hear the words. Do it as quickly as you can and then get back to where you were.

The class is out of control

In this case, use a calming activity like telling a story or filling in the words in a text which you read to the whole class. This means that you always have to have what you might call 'emergency activities' ready – activities that you can use in situations like this. When in doubt, pick up a reading book.

An activity is taking too long

You can:
  a) say that the pupils can do this activity so well already that you want to move on,
  b) ask the pupils to finish it for homework,
  c) say you'll come back to it another day (and then you must remember to do so),
  d) decide that this activity is so important that you want to spend time on it. This means adjusting the lesson plan for the next time.

You have extra time

If you have time left over, then you can use one of your emergency activities mentioned earlier, but remember to choose one that suits the mood of the class, and try to adapt it so that it fits in with what you've been doing. Of course, you can always say to the pupils, 'All right, today you've been so clever that we're going to play a game, or listen to a story, or add to our rhyme book.' That leaves you free to do whatever you want.

An activity doesn't work

If, for example, the cassette player doesn't work, don't spend time trying to get it to work. Leave it and read the text or sing the song yourself. If for some reason you can't, tell the pupils, 'The cassette player isn't working. Let's do something else.' If a game isn't working out, finish off the activity as soon as you can and move on to something else. Don't try to repair or change things like this in the middle of a lesson.

An activity is too difficult

If an activity doesn't work because the language is too difficult for the pupils, stop it gently and move on to an easy activity which you know they can do: 'Well, this is very difficult, and you've done very well. Let's move on to something else now.'

Questions and activities

1 Look at the long term plans on page 99. Can you
   make a similar plan for a class you have had or will have? If
   you don't have a class, look at one of the textbooks and make
   a long term plan from that.
2 Look at the short term plan on page 101. Keeping in mind
   what we said about topic-based teaching in Chapter 7, try to
   make up your own short term plan for a different topic.
3 On page 102, point 6, we mentioned that you should balance
   your lessons. Go through the lesson plans on pages 102 and
   103 checking for all four points. Is there room for
   improvement here?
4 In the section on what to do when things go wrong, we talked
   about having to have emergency activities like story telling.
   What other activities might be useful in emergencies? What
   do your colleagues do?

The tools of the trade

In this final chapter, we've tried to put together a collection of materials which we think you will find useful in your teaching situation. Since the physical world is the main means of conveying meaning to young children, a wide variety of teaching aids is necessary in the foreign language classroom. Lessons will be much easier and much more exciting for the children if you make full use of things and objects as well as language to get your meaning across.

Materials for you and your pupils to make

Puppets

These can be paper bag puppets, glove puppets, hand puppets or finger puppets. In addition to the actual puppets a simple 'stage' is very useful if you want to perform dialogues and sketches.

Class mascot

We've used Teddy as our class mascot, but you might like to have a rag doll or a special puppet or something of local significance.

Paper dolls

These are very useful for teaching clothes, but have quite a short life and have to be regularly replaced.

English corner

We said quite a lot about this in Chapter 2, and, of course, the basics have to be there already – the board, the shelves, etc., but encourage pupils to collect anything which is in any way connected with the English-speaking world. Displays should not be permanent.

Cardboard boxes

Collect shoe boxes and all other sorts of boxes for filing – ones with lids are more useful. The boxes can be covered with paper, decorated and labelled. Make a couple of new ones for each class – partly because the boxes get a bit worn after a while, and partly because classes like to think they have their own boxes. Boxes can also be used as building bricks to make shops, houses, castles, forests, etc.

Picture cards

These can be drawings or cut-outs from magazines, or perhaps photos. It is easiest to sort these according to size – really big ones for class work, and smaller ones for individual/pair/group work. Once you've sorted them for size, put them into themes or subject areas, like 'people', 'places', 'food', etc. .

Card games

Almost all card games can be made into language card games and while you want to concentrate on games where some sort of language interaction is taking place, you can also play card games simply for relaxation. Games like 'Memory' can be played without saying a word, but if you use cards like this, then at least recognition is taking place:

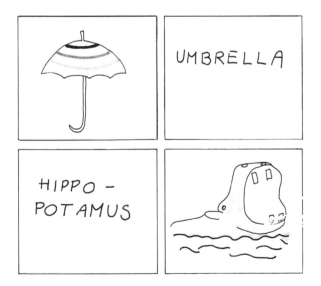

Here is an example of Happy Family cards made by a couple of girls in their third year of learning English:

Board games

Older children (and teachers) can make up all sorts of board games. Not only are board games useful for relaxation and/or language work, but the making of them presents a real challenge. Most children have played board games of some sort at home, and you can get wonderful language work out of making up the rules. You can make board games for almost any subject. For example, you can make up obstacle board games on topics like 'travelling through the jungle' or 'a fantastic birthday':

Word/Sentence cards

Word cards are useful for displays and for work on the flannelgraph. Sentence cards should only be used for the beginners and only with sentences which are used a lot. If you want to get full use out of your collection, you should work out a system of classification.

Here are a couple of suggestions of display systems for word cards and sentences which you can make yourself:

Word card displays   (Flexible order)

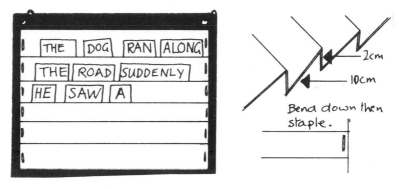

Word displays   (Inflexible order)

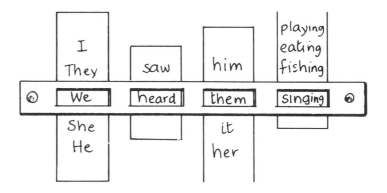

These examples of word card displays are taken from Andrew Wright's *Visual Materials for the Language Teacher*.

Books/Reading cards

We talked about these in the chapter on reading, and we look at the organisation of your books on pages 112 and 113.

Transparencies

If you have an overhead projector, then some of your pictures and other material can be copied onto transparencies. Transparencies should be kept in special plastic covers or framed and then put into a file. They keep well, take up very little space and are very useful for working with the whole class.

Calendar

Your calendar should show the date, the day, the weather and birthdays/special days.

Clock

Very simple clocks with movable hands are invaluable in the language classroom, not only for telling the time as in the exercise on page 37, but also for setting the scene and changing time from the here and now.

Materials to buy

Readers

If we were to choose only one of the teacher's aids listed in this chapter, easy readers and children's books in English would be our choice, and we feel it is better to have lots of different ones rather than class sets. Readers are a real investment for the language learner, and so we want to look in a bit more detail at how to put your books in order.

Coding

Although it is tempting to code books according to difficulty, we would not advise it, since we think that children should select books they *want* to read, and not the ones that the teacher says they are ready to read. So try to find some other way of organising your books, such as by subject matter – 'animals', 'fairy stories', 'facts'. This means, of course, that the teacher has to read through all the books first, select and classify. This is the type of activity which can be done usefully with other teachers or with the school librarian.

Displaying the books

Put the books on low open shelves if at all possible or in clearly marked boxes in your English corner. You might want to put new books or books which lots of people seem to be reading on low tables. Or you might put the books in book pockets. The point is that however you arrange your books, you should try to make sure that the children are physically able to reach them.

Borrowing cards
Have a system so that you know who has each book and how long he or she has had it. You might have a large card inside each book, and when the pupil borrows it he or she writes his or her name and the date on the card and puts the card in the space left by the book. This not only lets you see who has the book, but also tells you how popular the book is. The card can be very simple, and the pupils can take turns at being the librarian and seeing that others fill in the cards.

The Nose Book		
Name	Date out	Date in
Sachiko	Aug 10	Aug 12

Maps

You should have a map of the world or a globe in the classroom. A map of your local area is also useful, especially if it shows rivers and mountains etc. clearly.

Wallcharts

There are a number of wallcharts on the market which are made for the language classroom. Be on the lookout for charts for other subjects too, especially if you are going to do theme work or take part in projects working across the curriculum.

Toys

Cars, animals, furniture, etc. There are endless uses for toys in the language classroom. They also help to connect the child's world outside the classroom to what is happening inside the classroom.

Building blocks

Lego is wonderful, but expensive. Other types of building blocks – wooden or plastic – are just as versatile, and can become anything from cakes to houses.

Cassette recorders

You should have at least one cassette recorder which can record in every classroom. There are reasonably cheap cassette recorders on the market which have built-in microphones. These are quite good enough for recording yourself and the children in the classroom.

Cassettes

Just as you can never have enough reading material, you can never have enough recorded material. Remember also to have blank cassettes to record in the classroom.

Overhead projector

Even though it will probably be up to someone else to decide whether or not to buy this kind of equipment, if you are asked if you need/want one, say 'yes'. Presenting materials on the overhead projector allows you to face the children all the time and provides the children with a common focus of attention. You can come back to the same material whenever you want to, and you can use the same material with different classes.

We have only mentioned two pieces of equipment here – the cassette recorder and the overhead projector. There are others which may be available to you – slide projectors, videos, computers. If this is the case, find out exactly how they work and what material is available to use with each particular machine. Then you can decide how useful they will be in your lessons.

Materials for you to collect

This section is just to remind you that children find all sorts of
uses for materials which might otherwise be thrown away.
These are things which can be used in making collages, making
puppets, decorating pictures/boxes, going shopping, telling
stories, counting, acting, miming, etc. – the list is endless. Our
suggestions are only to get you thinking. If we put down
everything you could collect to use in the classroom this book
would go on for another ten pages instead of ending on this one!

You can collect:
Yogurt cartons, assorted ribbons, old cards, postcards, cotton
reels, all sorts of paper – tissue paper, old wrapping paper,
wallpaper – stamps, coins, buttons, string, jars, empty packets
of all sorts, bits of material.

Questions and activities

1 Can you add any suggestions to our list of materials which
   you and your pupils can make to use in the English lessons?
   What other things do you think would be useful for classroom
   work?
2 What else would you add to our list of things to collect?

References

Wright, A 1976 *Visual Materials for the Language Teacher*
   Longman
Wright, A and Haleem, S 1991 *Visuals for the Language Classroom*
   Longman